ADVANCE PRAISE FOR
WASIM THE DREAM

Wasim has so much passion for the sport of natural bodybuilding. He has great potential, and I see him accomplishing even more in the future. His story is an inspiration for the younger generation of up-and-coming bodybuilders who strive to excel in the sport.

—Frank Zane, author, three-time Mr. Olympia and Mr. Universe, Hall of Fame bodybuilding and fitness icon

Wasim's energy is unbounded! His presence, dedication, and personality inspire others. I am honored to have been his mentor and watch him achieve success on his journey toward his dreams in fitness, education, and the corporate world.

—Eric the Trainer, The Celebrity Fitness trainer and icon, TV host and author

Wasim is a great face for the INBA as a natural athlete. I have watched him rise through the rankings with admiration. His integrity, excellence, dedication, and spirit exemplify the values of our organization. He continues to push himself and excel in the sport, representing not just himself but his family, country, and fans.

—Denny Kakos, INBA President and founder

Wasim is an energetic student, with a big vision to change the world. His enthusiasm is infectious, and he continues to relentlessly pursue his goals. Wasim and students like him continue the legacy of Ernest Rady, the founder of our business school, who believed that Rady students will positively impact the world through entrepreneurship and innovation.

—Robert Sullivan, Dean of the Rady Business School

Qualcomm is a world-class company. As such, it is not easy to get into. Wasim overcame numerous obstacles and his perseverance paid off with many opportunities. I admire his drive, dedication, and mindset. He never gives up. The stories in his book truly lit a fire in my own soul to pursue my dreams.

—Mohamad Assaf, Electrical Engineer at Qualcomm

WASIM
THE DREAM

The Relentless Pursuit of
Turning Dreams into Reality

WASIM HAJJIRI

Printed and bound in the United States of America
ISBN: 978-0-9998255-0-1

BONUS MATERIAL

Go to my website, www.wasimthedream.com, and register to get two amazing products!

You will receive:

1) The top strategies to accomplish your wildest dreams

It outlines:
1. How to set goals
2. How to get the best mentors
3. How to build massive confidence
4. How to build powerful beliefs
5. How to make big decisions

And much more!

2) A summarized program from my main course:

Empowering young professionals and students with the psychology and techniques to relentlessly pursue their dream job

It outlines:
1. How to define your dream job
2. How to build confidence and optimism
3. How to leverage recruiters
4. How to leverage networking
5. How to nail the interviews

And much more...

I dedicate this book to my mother and father.
May my father's soul rest in peace.

TABLE OF CONTENTS

INTRODUCTION

Today is the day! The INBA (International Natural Bodybuilding Association) Natural Olympia! The Olympics of fitness! The finale!

I am going back and forth between excitement and fear as I stand in the back room getting my pump on (a short pre-competition workout). Close by me stand the two men I am competing against for the gold medal. Today the Olympia world champion will be announced.

I have been waiting for this my whole life. I've spent the last ten years weight lifting and I've put in a solid year of extensive, focused training. It's unbelievable to me that I will be stepping out on this stage. I am living my dream.

I also have the flu. It came on strong a few days ago. It is the worst possible timing. But I keep telling myself, "A true champion can adapt to anything." I believe I can deal with this and win despite feeling so sick. The prejudging round occurred earlier this morning. The judges have already chosen the scores, so there isn't anything left to do but be my best and stand proudly on that stage.

I'm pumped up now and ready to go out. They start calling our names for the initial lineup. When we are called, we will each go out and do an individual posing routine, and then they will announce the placings.

I am the last person to be called out. As I place my foot on the stage, the fever kicks in and I feel dizzy. Somehow, my mind keeps me going. I step out on the stage, pose, and flex with everything in me. Even though the chills that accompany the fever make my body shake, I hold myself as best I can.

Finally, we are called to the middle of the stage and lined up. It's time for the placings to be announced.

They start with third place and move on to the first. The head judge announces, "Third place from the USA . . . Tom Keyburn!" The crowd claps wildly. Suddenly I feel like the whole room freezes and time stops. "Second place from Korea . . . Seungjoo Kim!!"

I can't believe it! Does this mean I won? I can't breathe until they say my name. "First place from the USA . . . Wasim Hajjiri!!"

The crowd goes wild! The first thing I do is look for my mother. She's sitting in the front row, smiling, laughing, and cheering from her heart. I spot a group of my friends screaming their hearts out for me! I am overcome with sheer ecstasy and happiness!

After receiving the medals, we are taken to the back for a one-on-one interview with INBA TV. The first question I'm asked is, "What does this win mean to you?"

I reply, "I'm representing Jordan. My mom traveled over eighteen hours to come to the Olympia. It's been a great journey and a great victory for my family."

I think to myself, *They need a sound bite for TV, but there is no time to tell my whole story.*

No sound bites can explain the years of hard work and dedication that got me here. It can't tell the story of how someone from Jordan flew thousands of miles and moved to the United States to build a new life. There's no way to document the endless frustrations and failures that I experienced in one sentence. My Olympia win was a true victory for me, and it wasn't just about the gold medal. It was about my country, my mom, my friends, my team, and everyone around me who helped me. It was about following my dreams and taking steps toward my vision every day. This is the story I want to share with you.

THE BIKE RACE
DOING WHAT IT TAKES TO WIN

My father married my mother late in his life. She was his second wife, and he already had eight children from his first wife. Subsequently I have around twenty nieces and nephews, most of whom are close to my age. Because my brothers and sisters are all much older than me, I grew up spending a lot of time with my nieces and nephews.

My parents and I lived on an olive farm on the outskirts of Amman. Besides olive trees, we had animals: horses, chickens, dogs, cats, ducks, sheep, and goats. Every Friday all the members of the family who lived in Jordan would gather on the farm to spend the day together. There was always delicious food, conversation, and laughter. My older brothers and sisters would spend time with my dad while I occupied myself by running around the farm with my cousins, nieces, and nephews.

We would swim in the pool or play basketball and soccer in the playing field. We'd play tag through the orchards and around the garden where my dad grew much of our food. We'd play with the horses in the barn and ride them in the corral. Or, we'd race our bikes on the long straight road that led from the gate to the house.

Pokémon cards, marbles, and video games were the currency that funded our outdoor competitions.

5

I had a large collection of Pokémon cards, but there was one special golden Charizard card that was impossible to get. One Friday, my cousin Laith announced that he had won this coveted Charizard card while playing marbles with kids in his neighborhood.

Me with our goats

Me with our horse

I *had* to have that card.

And there was no way he would give it to me.

After intense debate, we finally agreed to a bike race. If I won, he would give me the golden card. If he won, I had to give him 50 of my Pokémon cards, including 20 of the blue cards, which were very valuable as they were just one level below the gold cards.

I was determined to win. Laith was very fit and very fast on the bike. He picked the bike race because he knew he was good. But I was willing to do anything to win that card.

We picked a 200-meter stretch of dirt road to have our race. My nephew Saif would be the judge. He stood at the finish line. Laith's twin sister, Jumana, stood at the starting line to count off the race. As we stood at the starting line, Laith and I used our hands and feet to try to knock the other off balance, hoping the other would fall.

Jumana started counting. One . . . Two . . .

Right before she could say three, Laith took off!

"Cheater!" I shouted. He laughed back at me. He fully intended to win the race, keep his beloved card, and get 50 of mine.

I had a lot on the line!

I blasted off at full speed and went crazy on the pedals! By the 150-meter mark I couldn't feel my legs anymore. Everything in me was telling me to stop and give up, but nothing mattered more at that moment than winning. As we neared the finish line, Laith and I were head to head. I gained some speed and started to pull ahead.

Suddenly there was a loud "boom." A nail punctured my tire, causing me to lose control of my bike! Like a slow-motion cartoon, I flew off my bike and into a nearby tree. I had no serious injuries, but I was covered in scratches.

Because of the accident, we agreed to call off the competition. I brushed myself off. We all laughed about it and continued on with our play. I didn't win the card that day, but I was still determined to get it somehow.

Some weeks later, after multiple negotiations and even some fighting, we came to an agreement. I gave him 100 of my cards, including 50 blue ones. And he gave me the prized Charizard gold card! I finally had it! Now *I* was the one showing it off and bragging that I had gotten it!

Me and my cousin Laith

KEY TAKEAWAY

My goal was to get the Charizard card. My opponent was tough. The stakes were high, and the road to the goal involved a race that would be bumpy.

I fell and failed to win. I got bruises and scratches. Laith wouldn't give up the card without a fight. I changed my approach and raised the stakes. It worked, and I got the Charizard gold card.

What I learned from that experience was that whenever I aim for a big goal, I have to be willing to do whatever it takes, including giving my all, taking big risks, and failing.

When I failed, changing my approach and persisting allowed me to push forward and overcome whatever challenges and obstacles came my way. In the end, when I win, the joy of victory is amazing and makes the struggle worth it.

REMEMBER...

Whenever you aim for a big goal,
you have to be willing to do whatever it takes.

THE BLUE LUNCH BOX

THE POWER OF FIGHTING
FOR YOUR BELIEFS

School wasn't a friendly place for me. While I had close friends, there were also bullies. I was shorter than most of the kids, and being chubby didn't help either.

In fourth grade, Omar was one of these bullies. His blond hair folded over a buzz cut around his ears and neck. He was taller and stronger than me. Omar was the cool kid in school. The one all the girls liked.

He ridiculed me over my lunch box. By that grade all the students packed their lunch in their backpacks, but I loved my old blue tin lunch box and used it every day.

At the end of class one day as I was making my way to the parking lot to get picked up, Omar marched over to me and with a mocking smile, said, "Hey, Wasim, why don't you put some diapers in that ugly lunch box of yours and bring them with you to school tomorrow?"

I got so angry, my heart started pounding and my face turned blood red. I couldn't take it anymore.

I held the lunch box aloft and slammed it down on his arm with all my strength.

He pushed me in retaliation, and I fell to the ground. I immediately jumped back up again and punched him in the face hard.

9

I saw my father in the distance getting out of the car to pick me up. I wanted to impress him, so I started punching harder.

My dad came running toward us to stop the fight. He pulled us apart and held us away from each other.

Even though he was holding me back, I was still throwing punches in the air and kicking. Finally, I calmed down and walked back to the car with my dad. I had bruises on my face and arms.

As soon as we were both back in the car, my father turned to look at me. I thought, *Uh oh, I'm definitely in big trouble.*

He paused for a second . . . then broke out laughing.

"You really put up a good fight out there, son. I'm proud of you."

I smiled and asked him, "So you're not mad at me?"

He smiled at me and said, "Let me tell you a story about when I was your age."

My father was born in 1929. He grew up in the post–World War I economic recession. He was the oldest in a family of five brothers and five sisters.

"When I was ten years old, World War II began, and my world was in complete chaos. My father was elderly and unwell. I had to learn to hustle in order to earn a living. I worked day and night transporting his merchandise from city to city in order to provide for the family.

"With no car, I rode my horse and was at constant risk of being robbed. I learned how to be tough and survive in the worst situations.

"One day," he explained, "my family had completely run out of food. I had to make an emergency trip from Amman [the capital of Jordan] to Madaba [another city in Jordan]. I planned to exchange a bundle of wool for food.

"It was a cold winter night and the road was long. As the horse walked along the road, I put my head down on the horse's neck, using the bag of wool as my pillow. I dozed off for a few minutes.

"Suddenly the horse stopped. I woke up to find a large man grabbing the bag of wool out of my arms as he ran off.

"I jumped off the horse and started running after the thief. There was no way I was going to let that bag get away. Your uncles and aunts were young and starving.

"I gained on the thief, jumped on his back, and started punching him, but he was too strong.

"He threw me roughly to the side and continued running. Even though I landed on rocks and was hurt, I got up again and started chasing after him at full speed using every last ounce of strength that I had.

"After thirty minutes, the thief finally stopped running. He looked back, and when he noticed me still running after him, he got scared.

"We got into a heavy fistfight and I took many punches. Even with blood all over my face, I didn't give up. Finally I snatched the bag and started running back to my horse, hoping it hadn't been stolen in my absence. The thief, thankfully, gave up. I made it to Madaba, where I exchanged the wool for food and turned around without resting or eating to head back home.

"When I finally arrived home, I was exhausted, bruised, and bloody. But my family had food to eat."

He ended the story with this advice: "Son, whoever or whatever hits you, make sure you hit back harder, and never give up."

This one phrase from my father stuck in my heart. After Omar, I got into other fights as well. We all know there are many bullies in the world. My father instilled the strength in me to always stand my ground and fight back with all my power. I never let anyone step on my pride, no matter who it was.

My father was the oldest in his family. At eight years old, my grandfather used to let him work, and when he became ill, my father was the man of the house. When he came of age, he got a business education, learned English, and got a job in accounting. Eventually he built a company that became one of the top in Jordan in his industry. His life was an interesting one. He traveled the world and learned about international business to expand his knowledge. A great quality that my dad had was to live simply and be humble, and he taught us these same values. Because he worked so hard from an early age, he instilled hard work and dedication into my heart, and as I grew older, I always tried to match his work ethic.

My father married twice. My mom was his second wife. He already had eight children from his first wife. I was my mother's only child.

Dad was tough and very strict on my siblings and me. He wanted us to develop the strength and resilience to deal with any situation. He always told me, "Life is hard and will constantly change, and you have to be tough." He taught me discipline, hard work, and dedication from an early age. I didn't quite understand it at that time, but as I grew up, I certainly benefited from his approach.

My dad is the godfather of our family and at the top of the family tree. He worked very hard to make sure that all of us were taken care of emotionally and financially. He also required his children to work very hard and earn whatever they needed.

Anyone who had a problem came to him for a solution. He was widely respected in the communities of Amman. In Jordan, we have an old tradition of kissing the hands of our elders and parents. This shows love and respect. From the youngest to the oldest in our family, whenever we entered a room where my father was, we would immediately walk up to him and kiss his hand. He would respond with "God bless you."

My father had ten younger siblings, two wives, nine children, and twenty grandchildren. The whole family idolized him and depended on him. He was an amazing person for us to look up to. He sacrificed so much to provide a good life for all of us. I have often wondered, "How the heck did he manage to handle all of that?" He was truly a warrior.

He had many responsibilities, but I didn't fully understand that when I was a child. The age difference between us made it hard for me to connect with him at times. Most of the conversations he engaged in didn't make much sense to me. He would converse on politics, business, and deep life lessons. As a child, I was more interested in playing Mortal Kombat on my PlayStation 1. He started teaching me lessons in the form of stories like the one he told me after I got into a fight. I didn't understand him well when I was young, but as I matured, I started to appreciate him more and learn from him.

My father: The godfather of the Hajjiri family

KEY TAKEAWAY

My father taught me from an early age to always fight back. As an adult, I have experienced many situations in which something or someone wanted to take me out or knock me down. I had to stand my ground, fight, and never give up. I never backed down from a fight. When I fought back, I used all my power to do so.

I believe that fighting back is required to survive and excel in this world. I am not talking about physical fighting, but about fighting in the face of problems and difficult situations. I am determined to win, no matter what. We all know that life tends to be challenging, but I believe we have the power to win if we fight back with all our heart and soul.

I leave you with this quote to write down and memorize:

Whoever or whatever hits you,
make sure to hit back harder and never give up!

MENTORS

HOW THEY PUSH YOU TO ACHIEVE YOUR DREAMS

S tudying wasn't my thing. I often struggled with my grades. The second I got home from school, I threw my backpack down and went outside to play. My backpack would stay untouched until I opened it the next day in class.

Saturday detention was part of my monthly routine. The school would frequently call my parents complaining about my grades, or that I was missing classes and frequently late to class. I did the bare minimum to pass my courses.

One time in class, I was daydreaming about playing basketball and riding my bike around the farm.

My daydreams were interrupted by a sneeze. I had a game I played with my friends called "Ceiling." Whenever you sneezed, someone would call out "ceiling," and you had to quickly jump up and touch the ceiling. Otherwise whoever called it would punch you on the arm five times.

After someone in class sneezed, one of my friends called out "Ceiling!" I immediately jumped up out of my seat and punched the ceiling. Unfortunately, the ceiling tile cracked and fell on my desk in several pieces. There was dust and debris everywhere. It was a huge mess.

The whole class cracked up and started laughing. The teacher turned around and observed the mess. At first his face registered shock, then it turned red and he yelled, "Wasim, get out of my class right now!" My hair and face were full of dust and debris, but I found the situation funny too, so I started laughing as I walked out the door.

After washing off the dust in the restroom, I walked toward the principal's office. I was afraid of what the principal was going to do. *Am I going to be expelled? This is so humiliating. What am I going to tell my parents?*

I walked into the principal's office with my shoulders slumped and sadness on my face. I had to explain what happened in class.

The principal had seen quite a lot of me by this time, as I was sent to her office at least once a month either for fights with bullies or for some other school-related infraction. After listening to my account of events, she warned me, "If you continue at this pace, Wasim, you will be expelled from this school permanently."

My punishment was to spend a whole week taking first-grade classes so that I would learn that what I did was childish. At 15 years old, sitting with the first graders for a week would be humiliating.

But I didn't care about that. What concerned me more was what my mom's reaction would be.

My mom always stressed the importance of education, and she needled and nagged me daily to push myself to study hard so I would graduate. Her mantra was, "Education is the most powerful tool you can have while going through life. Always strive to get the best knowledge."

She was the oldest of her three sisters, and my grandfather's right hand in his business ventures. At a very early age he used to take her to his meetings and she traveled with him while he did business around the country. He was very tough on her, but he taught her how to be strong. She learned fast and helped him while my grandmother took care of her sisters.

As a young woman, her dream was to become a graphic designer.

My mom was one of the best students in her class. After high school, she got a full scholarship to attend the Fashion Institute of Technology, which is one of the top universities in New York in graphic design. She valued education and worked hard for it.

Her father, however, was very attached to her. Out of his three daughters, she was the favorite.

When she got the acceptance letter for college in New York, she was too afraid to tell him at first, although the news was all over her school. Her teachers and the principal were so proud that one of their students would be going abroad to represent their school.

She was very excited and started planning for college abroad. When she finally told her father, he refused to let her go. His decision was final, and there was no room for negotiation.

She was devastated and didn't speak with him for weeks. Ultimately, she sacrificed her educational dreams to remain in Jordan by her father's side.

By staying in Jordan, she actually started working with my father at his company, and that's how they met. She then became his right arm in the company, and they eventually got married.

Some years later she developed another dream. She would have a son and devote her life to raising him to be the best in the world at whatever he did. That dream came true for her when I was born. Ever since I was a baby, she supported me and pushed me to do my best. Having started to work at a young age, she was very hardworking and driven. She wanted to make sure I grew up with the same work ethic she had. But studying wasn't my thing.

My mother and me

I knew it was painful for my mom to watch how I struggled in school and with my grades, but I felt incapable of making any significant change. In high school, we used the GCE system. This is the educational system used in England, and it was very advanced. We took SAT-level English in eighth grade, and by twelfth grade, we were doing college-level subjects.

In tenth grade, news spread throughout our school that they were bringing in one of the best teachers in Jordan to teach us physics. This teacher, Nabil, was well liked by all his students in past schools and had a great reputation.

Nabil walked into our first physics class with a big smile on his face. It was the kind of smile that made you feel good about yourself.

The second he started explaining the class material, I could feel the excitement and enthusiasm he had for the subject. I found myself actually paying attention in class—a new experience for me. I started to realize that this might be the first time in my entire school life when I was excited about a subject. My backpack was opened after school, and what a shock . . . I did my homework!

Nabil, my high school teacher

As the semester passed, I developed a good relationship with Nabil. I discovered that he had to drive almost two hours each way in order to get to and from our school. This amazed me. It showed me that he cared about teaching.

One day after class I went up to him and asked him, "Mr. Nabil, how come you are always happy?" He started laughing and told me, "You know, everyone asks me the same question."

Nabil was passionate about life and loved his family. He always talked about his wife and his child. He carried a very positive attitude and made everyone around him smile.

He was such a contrast to my previous teachers.

He advised us to start taking a vitamin called Centrum. He told us it would change our lives and help get us good grades. I believed him, so I started to take the vitamin and expected to get better grades.

He instructed us to wake up at 7:00 a.m. on weekends so we could finish all our homework and then still have plenty of time to enjoy the weekend. I started waking up early to study. This was another first for me. My parents were surprised and delighted.

Nabil, my high school teacher

Nabil's influence shifted my entire psychology around education. Slowly but surely my grades started to improve, and the school started calling my parents about my improvements instead of my failures. It was a nice change. Even though he didn't mentor me directly, his positive attitude had a great effect on me.

I started to dream about becoming an engineer. I saw engineers as people who changed the world through technology, and I wanted to be a part of that.

To get into the top engineering universities, an average of 85% was needed in the GCE exams.

By the beginning of twelfth grade, I averaged in the low 70s. The only way for me to get my score up to 85% was to repeat six subjects—a total of twelve exams to study for. This seemed an impossible goal.

I talked to Nabil. He referred me to a great tutor who had an attitude similar to his so that I could keep up the positive energy.

Between the tutor and Nabil, I started to believe in myself and believe that it was possible for me to become an engineer. I started to push myself, and it was working. My grades were soaring.

My biggest challenge would be the finals. If I wanted to get into a top engineering school, I had to pass twelve exams with at least 85%, all within a two-week period. I couldn't screw up any of the exams.

The last two months before exams I pretty much locked myself in my room. I studied day and night. I didn't see any of my friends, and hardly even saw my parents. My tutor at that point was my best friend.

I hunkered down and prepared myself for the upcoming war—the finals.

Finals week began. I was stressed and tired due to lack of sleep, but I smelled victory and felt the door to my dream was nearby. I was ready to be the last man standing on the battlefield.

Chemistry was my number-one enemy, and it was the final exam. I walked into the auditorium where the exam was held with sheer willpower and determination. Even though I was scared and stressed out of my mind, my preparation held my emotions together.

They had teachers patrolling each line of desks, walking up and down making sure no one could cheat. It was intense.

Three and a half hours into the four-hour exam, I looked at the big clock in the middle of the room. I still had five questions left. Usually each question took me ten minutes. I started to freak out. *Will I make it? Oh no, I'm screwed!*

Sweat started pouring down my face, and my heart started to race. I was writing like a madman. With five minutes left, I was down to one final question. That question covered material I wasn't confident in, but I didn't give up. Ideas came to me, and I wrote them down without hesitation.

"Time is up!" they called. I put down my pencil and breathed a sigh of relief. I was finished. It was over! I was very proud of myself for giving it my all. I considered it a major victory in a very tough battle.

A month later my grades arrived in the mail. I was scared to open the envelope. I stared at it for nearly thirty minutes, imagining what would happen if I failed.

How would I tell my dad? How would I tell the tutor and Nabil? This was the first time I'd ever studied this hard, and to fail would feel like death to me.

Screw it! I thought to myself. *Whatever happens—so be it!*

With a pounding heart I opened the envelope. I quickly scanned each individual grade, searching for the total.

There it was! 85.1%!

WOW! I did it! I thought to myself.

I started running around the room like a madman, jumping on the furniture and screaming. My endorphin levels soared through the roof, and I felt sheer ecstasy and joy.

All of my jumping around caused a kind of earthquake for my parents downstairs. They heard me screaming and came running upstairs.

"I passed! I passed! I passed!" I screamed.

They started jumping around and celebrating with me. It was an amazing celebration not only for me but also for them, as they had put up with all the crazy things that I did at school.

Graduating from high school seemed impossible to me until I met Nabil. Under his influence, I broke through the mental limits that I had subconsciously built for myself. After putting in the work and achieving the desired result, I began to believe in myself and believe that I could do anything if I set my mind to it.

KEY TAKEAWAY

Nabil had such a positive effect on my education. Although he wasn't mentoring me one on one, his influence was still very powerful. With his positive attitude and energy, he managed to shift my whole psychology about studying and school. Nabil also tapped into a network of other teachers who helped me with other subjects so I could pass those as well.

If it weren't for Nabil, I probably wouldn't have graduated from high school and would have continued failing. Mentors are the number-one thing I look for when pursuing any goal. A mentor will see things in me that I cannot see myself. They will push me to work harder. They help me believe in myself and my abilities. I also learn from all their experience and save time and years of trial and error by myself.

One simple thing that a mentor says can change your whole life.

REMEMBER...

Having a mentor is the most powerful tool to have when pursuing any goal. I learned that one person can change your whole life.

HOW FRIENDS AND ENEMIES HELP US ACHIEVE OUR GOALS

After graduating from high school, I had to decide which university I would attend. In the Jordanian culture, young people don't leave home at the age of eighteen. They live with their parents, who provide for them financially until they graduate from college, get a job that will allow them to support themselves, and eventually get married.

I wanted to be independent and to carve my own path after high school, and studying abroad was the best solution. Since we used the British system in our high school, it was easy to get accepted into universities in England.

A year before graduation our school had us initially apply to different schools in England, but now it was time to finalize the process and pick the university we wanted to attend.

Engineering programs in British universities took three years to complete instead of the usual five. It made a lot of sense for me to attend a university in Britain. Another important reason for me was that all my friends had plans to go there.

I applied to several British universities and started to get excited about moving to another country. I researched cities to visit, tourist attractions, and mapped out a whole plan for my first semester.

I just assumed my parents would be okay with me studying abroad.

High school best friends

The day we had the conversation, I sat them both down and showed them the applications I had sent in. I did my best to sell them on the schools and the idea of me studying abroad.

As far as my dad was concerned, there was no discussion. I was not leaving.

I kept at it, trying to convince them. To no avail.

I finally asked my dad, "Why? Why won't you let me go?"

He responded, "You're still just a kid. You're not mature enough. You're not ready."

There was nothing I could do to convince him otherwise.

I wasn't ready to give up. So I lobbied with all of my friends' parents. I had them call my parents to try to convince them.

Eventually I realized it wasn't going to happen. I was crushed.

What made it especially difficult was that all my friends were leaving to study abroad in schools in England, Canada, or the US. I would be the only one from our graduating class of twenty to stay in Jordan for college. I felt left behind, and I desperately wanted to be independent and live my own life.

At the time, I didn't agree with my parents' decision, but looking at it now, I realize they were right. I still wasn't mature enough.

I know that staying in Jordan for college was an important factor in my growth, and it turned out to be the best decision. It was a tough pill to swallow, but I decided to adapt and look for the good.

I got into Princess Sumaya University for Technology, one of the best universities in Jordan. It has worldwide recognition and accreditation.

In the first semester, a tall, bulky guy named Muath was in some of my classes. That summer I had worked hard in the gym and grown stronger and bigger. Luckily for me, I'd had a good growth spurt, so I was taller and stronger than the short, chubby kid that I had been in high school. I had much more confidence.

Whenever I looked at Muath, he seemed to be talking about me to the people he was with. I felt a lot of hostility from him. He clearly didn't like me, and I had no idea why. It was odd, but I didn't care much about him or what he thought. We never spoke, but whenever we'd pass each other in college, it was very awkward.

I was finding my way around during my first semester. I was entering a new world as an outsider. Most of the other students in my cohort had existing friendships from high school, whereas all my high school friends were studying abroad.

The first couple of weeks I did my best to ignore Muath's behavior. But a few months in, people started coming up to me and telling me, "Hey, Wasim, Muath is saying bad things about you."

I was shocked. My initial response was, "What is wrong with this guy?" I decided that the mature thing to do would be to ignore him and not care too much about what he or anyone else said about me.

One day I was minding my own business, walking to a book shop across the street from the university with a friend. My friend went in to get a book and I waited for him outside. I saw Muath walking toward me. I immediately felt that something bad was about to happen.

He walked right up to me, leaned in close to my face, and forcefully said, "What's your problem, kid?" and pushed me.

I had a notebook in my hand, which I immediately threw at him, and threw a punch to his face. He punched me back, and the fight was on. People gathered around us, including some of Muath's friends. Some were trying to stop the fight, and some were looking on and cheering, just like a boxing match. It was brutal and he was tough.

As Muath and I were pulled away from each other, he shouted, "It's not over! I'm going to meet you here after classes and we will continue what we started." I screamed back, "I'll be here, waiting for you!"

By this time my heart was pounding and adrenaline was rushing through my veins. I was excited to continue the fight and prove myself. Muath was very tough, but I had put up a good fight. By the time we were pulled off each other, my shirt was ripped and bloody.

Muath's friends had gathered by then, and I knew he would come back with them. I needed reinforcements. I skipped my next class and started calling my friends from outside the university to come and help me.

There was one guy that I knew who was very tough: Yousef. No one in his neighborhood messed with him. Thankfully I had a great relationship with him, and he was a good friend of my cousin, who lived in his neighborhood.

I called him and explained the whole story. He agreed to help me, and he showed up after school with two other big, strong guys.

As the school emptied out, I waited patiently, looking around for Muath.

Finally, I saw him with his posse. He had a tall guy with him who was six foot four. I thought to myself, *Oh man, this is going to be rough.* As they walked toward us, my heart beat faster and I prepared myself to fight.

They all stopped about twenty feet away, and only the tall guy continued walking toward us. I walked up to him.

He said, "Wasim, I want you and Muath to settle this without a fight. Explain to me what happened."

It turns out that his name was Amer, and he was the leader of the pack which included Muath's friends, and he was known to be very peaceful. I explained the situation and what had happened.

He responded, "This is silly. We are all first-year students, and we should all be friends."

Yousef walked toward us too, started talking with Amer, and shook hands peacefully. Then my group and his group shook hands to make peace.

I came face to face with Muath. He presented his hand to me first, which was respectful by our cultural standards. I shook his hand, and that was it. It was settled.

Suhail, Assaf and me

Muath was apparently known to be tough, and no one messed with him or his group. He actually respected me for standing up to him.

The next day the news somehow spread all over school that I had stood up to Muath. Now people knew not to mess with me. As school progressed, Muath and I became good friends and we laugh about this story today.

I met two other guys who became my best friends, Mohammed Assaf and Suhail Romanos. I counted them as more than brothers; we were just like the Three Musketeers. We hung out all the time, always had fun, and supported each other.

KEY TAKEAWAY

After graduating from high school, I wanted to go to England, but my parents wouldn't let me go. They were right that I wasn't mature enough. Staying in Jordan forced me to grow. In this and other situations in life, when I aimed for a certain goal, I didn't always get exactly what I wanted, but the change in direction ended up being better and led to a better outcome.

When I stood up against Muath, he ended up respecting me and ultimately became my friend. Even though standing up to him meant getting punched in the face, kicked, and getting a bloody nose, it still ended up having a good result.

REMEMBER...

Sometimes not reaching the goal turns out
to be a better outcome and will cause you to
grow and will open up other opportunities.

USING "THE SECRET" TO VISUALIZE AND ACHIEVE MY GOALS

The first two years of college I had fun, partied, and didn't study well. My grades suffered, and I was nearing probation. I was falling into the same hole that I had gone through in high school. I was going down the wrong path.

I met one of my friends for coffee and told her everything I was going through. She suggested I watch a great documentary called "The Secret." I did so, and I learned about visualization, positive thinking, goal setting, and focusing your thoughts on the things you want instead of the things you don't want. Here is how I applied it.

Electronic communications   (B+)
Electronics II (A-)
Circuits II (B)
Micro - Economics (B-)
Electronics Lab (A-)

I wrote down the grades I wanted

31

Goals	Date (deadline)	Action plan	Purpose of the goal	Vision
Graduate and become an engineer	August 2013 (graduation day)	1) Get help from other students 2) Study on the weekend (revise notes and do homework) 3) Lock myself in my room for a week to study nonstop for an upcoming test	1) My new dream was to become an engineer and change the world through technology and innovation 2) Make parents proud 3) Gain income and financial security 4) Feel accomplished	I visualized myself on graduation day throwing my hat in the air, celebrating with my parents and friends
Study every week	Weekly progress	Study with someone else to make it fun	1) Learn the material 2) Be prepared for the exam	I wrote down the grades that I wanted and visualized seeing them online after the exam
Talk to the top students in the class to get help	Within the next two weeks (September 1– 25, 2009)	1) Call Mazen 2) Call Assaf 3) Call James 4) Meet with them at least once a month and go over material	1) Understand the material 2) Pass my exams 3) Make the study process more enjoyable	I visualized meeting with these students, understand-ing the material, acing the tests, and celebrating

I started this process and visualized these things every single day. Slowly my grades improved. I was amazed by the results. I watched "The Secret" over and over until I felt it was engraved on my mind.

That summer I took on my first job as a sales and procurement representative at a furniture company. Making my own income felt like a great accomplishment. It was also a big part of my growth and made me focus more on school, as I learned more discipline.

At the beginning of the third year, we started taking very complex subjects that moved us toward what we wanted to specialize in. I chose telecommunications.

Telecommunications is one of the biggest and fastest-growing industries in the world. The first iPhone 2G came out in 2007. Ten years and twelve evolutions later, we have the iPhone X. I was interested in learning how this technology worked and dreamed of changing the world through my ideas.

The classes were crazy Electronic communications, microprocessors, and other classes with names that are hard to spell. Our university had top professors who had many major publications to their name, and they had one simple rule: No mercy. It appeared to me that they wanted to push our thinking beyond what the normal human brain is capable of.

Out of a class of 50 students, 20 failed. That was the average.

The top student in our cohort was a mega-genius named Mazen.

Mazen had a full scholarship due to his amazing GPA. He was smart to the point that he would prove that a professor's theories were wrong. A team of five professors would take on the challenge to try to disprove his theories, but they couldn't.

He even made up his own simplified theories from summarizing the material, and he taught them to others. "Mazen's Rules," he called them.

People from all over the school would come to him, and he was generous enough to help them all.

Thankfully he was a close friend of mine. Following my game plan, I went to him and asked for help, and he didn't refuse. I used to meet with him weeks before the tests. Over and over I would meet him to go over material. I think I drove him crazy sometimes, but he continued to help me.

On my own, I sometimes had a hard time believing I could pass the test or succeed, and he would give me the push that I needed. When I felt stuck or thought I couldn't do it, Mazen acted as a motivator and gave me a great push whenever I needed it.

All through my third year up until graduation, Mazen tutored me and helped me through some of these tough classes. I owe my success to him.

Every class I took, I built a good relationship with the professors. I would show up for office hours. I would do extra work if necessary to always be on their good side. When grading time came around, they knew who I was, and that helped. When I was stuck with anything, I would simply go and ask them for help.

KEY TAKEAWAY

After watching "The Secret," I learned about goal setting, visualization, and focusing my thoughts and actions on the things I wanted instead of the things that I didn't want. I created a table that helped me articulate my vision and plan. Instead of focusing on why I was failing and not getting the grades that I wanted, I started to think of different ways in which I could get help, improve, and get excellent grades. That shift of focus changed the whole game for me.

Asking for help is such a valuable tool that I use for literally anything that I want to accomplish. I've known many people who needed help but wouldn't ask due to ego. They usually missed out on opportunities. It is my belief that asking for help shows strength and resourcefulness. If it wasn't for Mazen's help, I wouldn't have passed those hard subjects.

Asking for help is very powerful and shows strength and resourcefulness.

THE GRADUATION PROJECT

HOW PREPARATION LEADS TO SUCCESS

In my last year of engineering school I started working, training, and interning at Orange Telecommunications, which is a French international tech company that's one of the best in the world. I gained a lot of experience and applied many engineering concepts that I had learned in my studies. It was great to get a taste of what the real engineering world looks like. I really loved it and couldn't wait to graduate and work full-time.

The fifth and final year of engineering school had started. The only thing standing between me becoming an engineer was my graduation project.

For the graduation project, I had to come up with a technical idea that would solve a problem. Then I would find a team to develop the idea so that ultimately we could pitch the theoretical and practical concept to the professors.

I wanted to find a solution for hit-and-run situations, as well as car theft. You get hit, the responsible party runs, and you pay thousands of dollars to repair damage to your car.

For a team member, the first person I thought of was Assaf, one of my best friends who I met in my first year. He is very tech-savvy and a hard worker. I talked to him about the idea, and he loved it. We teamed up together.

37

After a month of brainstorming, we had a solid plan for a solution. To sum it up, if someone was trying to steal your car while it was parked, a text message would be sent to your phone warning you. If your car experienced a hit-and-run, the other car's information would automatically be sent to your phone, including the date and time of the accident. We would be implementing sensors, Bluetooth and GSM technology to create the theoretical and practical concepts of the solution.

We called it ACAR (automatic car accident report).

We pitched the concept to the top professor in the school, and he approved our project! Our journey began . . .

We had eight months to make the system ready, theoretically and practically. At the end of eight months, we would present our solution to a panel of three professors who would judge it and determine our final grade. We had to get a high passing grade in order to graduate.

It was a very complex project. The number-one thing that we focused on was getting people all over the school to help us. We even went to professors from other schools. We got many minds to assist us.

Finally, after eight months of hard work and dedication, the system was 100% functional and ready to present.

The day of the presentation arrived! My five-year journey in engineering school had finally come to its end. Hundreds of restless nights plus countless hours of studying had led up to this day.

In the next hour, the decision of whether or not I was going to become an engineer was going to be made.

The night before our presentation, Assaf and I barely slept, as we were rehearsing the presentation over and over. Assaf is the type of person who is a little pessimistic and he didn't expect the best results. Personally, I had a very powerful belief that we would succeed, so I did my best to lift him up and help him think positively.

I learned about the power of affirmations from the book *Think and Grow Rich*. Napoleon Hill simply states that saying positive phrases out loud with strong emotion can boost your confidence and make you believe in yourself. Since we both needed a successful outcome, we started chanting, "We will succeed! We will graduate! We will have an amazing and successful presentation." We said it over and over, maybe a hundred times, until it was engraved on our minds.

The presentation took place in an auditorium, and no one except the team and a panel of professors was allowed inside.

Right before the presentation, I spent thirty minutes pumping Assaf up with motivational encouragement. I encouraged him to focus only on the final result: which was us graduating and celebrating all over the campus. He started to shift from pessimism to excitement.

We were both mentally ready, and our preparation was strong. As we walked into the auditorium, I looked at Assaf and could see his face starting to turn red. The bag he held in his hand started to shake. He was scared.

I felt strong and confident. I had instilled the idea of succeeding so deep into my subconscious mind that I was beyond the point of no return.

The presentation began. They looked through our documentation and started by firing questions at us left and right. We answered most of them, but some were complicated and we didn't answer them well.

We were shaken after the first round of questions, but the next phase was a fifteen-minute presentation, which I was ready for. It was our last chance to seal the deal and impress the professors.

As we were about to start, one of the professors raised his hand and immediately stopped us. There was an awkward moment of silence in the room before he spoke.

"Gentlemen, as I was reading your documentation, I was very impressed by the strength and dialogue of the English language used. Therefore, I would like to hear your presentation in English, not in Arabic."

We had spent the last month preparing the presentation in Arabic. Presenting in Arabic was always the case for every graduation project. No one ever had to present in English.

We were both shocked. I didn't know what to say or do. I looked at Assaf, and he looked shaken and his face turned even redder. Sweat was pouring down his face.

We had about thirty seconds to wrap our minds around presenting in English before we had to begin. It was very intense.

We had originally split the presentation in half, where both of us spoke for seven minutes. Assaf had the first half.

He started the presentation . . .

For the first minute, he did fine presenting in English. But before long he started making up words and mixing the material. As he struggled to present in English, he looked over at me with pleading in his eyes.

I had heard him rehearse his part so many times that I knew it by heart, so I jumped in and continued the presentation.

The next 14 minutes were a blur, because I was so intensely focused. I presented with all my heart and soul. As we finished, I looked in the eyes of the professors and knew we had won them over.

They asked us to step out of the room for a fifteen-minute break so they could deliberate and make their final decision.

As we exited the auditorium, Assaf and I took a deep breath and relaxed. It was so intense that the adrenaline was still pumping through my veins.

The fifteen minutes felt like fifteen years.

Finally, they called us back inside. The professors had a very serious look on their faces. I panicked for a second, thinking, *Oh no! Did we fail?*

We sat in front of them and they started explaining our mistakes and what we could have done better. The only thing my brain was hearing was "Blah, blah, blah . . ." I kept thinking, *Come on, man! Just give me the result and stop blabbering!*

Graduation

WASIM THE DREAM

They went on like this for about ten minutes before coming to their conclusion.

"Gentlemen, we are really proud of your work. You did a great job. Congratulations! You are now officially engineers!"

YES! We shook their hands, thanked them, and left. As soon as we were out of the auditorium, we jumped all over the place and ran to the celebration area.

Now it was time for the Jordanian celebrations!

All our families and friends were waiting. Other students gathered as well, and everyone was clapping and cheering for us.

They lifted us up on their shoulders and paraded us around. I felt like a king up there, and everyone was looking at me, proud and smiling. My mom even got a special band to come all the way from Petra to play music.

We started performing the traditional Jordanian dabkeh dance, jumping and dancing around. The experience felt like a rock concert, and we were the stars.

I'll never forget the look in my parents' eyes as they saw me up there. They cheered their hearts out for me. That day was one of the best of my life, and I will never forget it.

After the celebrations were over, it hit me. I thought to myself, *Wow, I am now an engineer. My dream really came true!* All of the ups, downs, major setbacks, and insane hard work that I had invested in my education were worth it. This one moment, one day of celebration, made me forget all the past hardships. It was a great way to close the college chapter of my life.

KEY TAKEAWAY

From the graduation project, I learned that preparation is a major key to success. This is true of almost any goal. Because of our strong preparation, I could manage the sudden change successfully. It also showed me that situations change all the time, and I must be able to deal with whatever is in front of me. Speaking our affirmations out loud helped inspire us and keep us going. I use affirmations a lot. You can create them for any area of your life in which you feel less confident.

REMEMBER...

Preparation is a major key to success because situations might change and you have to deal with whatever is in front of you.

FINDING AND LOSING NINA
EXPRESSING FEELINGS VS. HOLDING THEM IN

One beautiful summer morning, I got a phone call from one of my old high school friends, who invited me to his house for a gathering. I was excited to go see some people who I hadn't seen in a while.

As soon as arrived, I saw a beautiful girl sitting in the corner. I immediately rushed over and sat next to her.

"Hi, my name is Wasim," I said nervously.

It was love at first sight for me. My heart started pounding and I started to sweat. I didn't even know what to say after that.

She sensed that I was nervous, so she started to joke around to break the ice. Then I finally relaxed and began to have a normal conversation with her. We had a crazy connection and clicked right away.

Shortly after that, my friend walked in the room and came toward me. I thought that he was coming to say hi to me. He passed right by me and hugged Nina. He told her, "Hi, Babe. I see you met Wasim!"

She was actually his girlfriend. I felt like someone had punched me in the face. I got up, gave him a hug, and casually walked away to see other people.

After that party, I couldn't stop thinking about Nina, but I couldn't do anything about it.

I started to hang out with my friend more often, and Nina always showed up. She and I became close friends.

It was hard for me to ignore my emotions, because every time I saw her, I badly wanted to tell her how I felt. I felt like I was about to explode, but sucked it up and kept myself in the friend zone.

Five years passed, and I had not opened up to her about how I felt. I had ignored my feelings for her for so long, I eventually got used to it. I felt the pain of jealousy when I saw her in another relationship, but I had resigned myself to the fact that I had missed my chance.

The last semester before graduation, I met a girl named Clara. Clara was also Nina's friend. In a short time, Clara and I grew to like each other and started dating. Slowly Nina's attitude toward me started to change. She started to act differently. I began to wonder, "Does she like me? Or does she really dislike Clara for some reason?"

One day Nina and I decided to go for a drive. She told me, "I have something really important to tell you."

She paused for a minute and her eyes got teary.

"I have feelings for you!" she said softly. "That's why I can't see you with Clara!" She then burst into tears.

I was shocked. It only took a few seconds before the floodgates opened. I had five years of feelings buried deep and waiting to be expressed. I told her everything I felt for her. I told her how attracted I was to her from the second I met her five years earlier. I told her how every time I saw her with someone else, my heart felt like it was going to break, and how many times I wanted to tell her I loved her. I went on and on.

She was shocked that I had never mentioned anything. I told her how many times I wanted to but never found the right time.

I was beyond happy and relieved that this moment had finally come.

We talked for hours. It felt like a dream.

Only when I got home did I start to think about Clara. How would I explain all of this to her? I spent all night thinking about it.

I knew it was going to be painful, but I had to do it. Two days later I met with Clara and told her everything that had happened. She didn't take it well at all, and there were hours of crying and drama that I had to deal with.

I felt bad for doing this to Clara. It is something I regret. Because I didn't take action earlier in being honest with Nina, I ended up causing myself and others pain.

This is how I came to be with the woman of my dreams, Nina. It was now the beginning of my fairy-tale summer.

Nina and I took trips to all the tourist spots around Jordan. We went to the Dead Sea (one of the most well-known and famous tourist attractions). The Dead Sea is nine times saltier than the ocean. It has no fish and is salty to the point that you can float while reading a magazine. The sea produces a type of mud that people spread on their bodies and faces because it is good for the skin.

Close to the Dead Sea is Wadi Al Mujib, which is a great place for hiking. We hiked through mystic tunnels and pathways that dated back hundreds of years.

Mount Nebo: The Memorial of Moses, a Christian holy place

The rod of Moses

A short drive led us to the site where Jesus was said to have been baptized. The area is called "The Baptism Site." Close to this area is Mount Nebo, where the famous Saint John the Baptist Church is located. There is a monument to the rod of Moses that he used to part the sea.

Jerash

I also took Nina to the historic city of Jerash. It is one of the best places to have a nice dinner during the week. We ate dinner by candlelight at a historic restaurant with a view of ruins that date back to the Roman Empire.

Covered in mud at the Dead Sea

The Dead Sea

Saint John the Baptist Church

Jerash

Petra

Wadi Al Mujib

Map for the Baptism Site

Petra is one of the seven wonders of the world and is truly one of the most amazing places you will ever see. Hollywood movies like *Transformers: Revenge of the Fallen* and *Indiana Jones and the Last Crusade* were filmed there. Every time I visit Petra, I admire the architecture and the sheer size of the monuments. "How did these people design all of this thousands of years ago with nothing but basic tools?" I wondered.

As Nina and I enjoyed our summer in a fairy-tale bubble of love, we didn't think much about the long-term future of our relationship. If we had, we would have had to consider that her parents were working and living in Saudi Arabia. Because she was the type of person who always supported them, it meant that she'd eventually have to go back, which is what happened at the end of summer.

We decided to stay together and try out a long-distance relationship.

It was fine for the first couple of weeks, but then everything started to fall apart. We missed each other terribly and expressed it as anger and frustration, which negatively affected our relationship.

Soon enough, the relationship ended. We couldn't handle the long-distance aspect of things. It was too hard. I was crushed. I had been waiting five years for this to happen, and now it had all gone away.

For weeks, I was depressed. I barely ate and didn't talk to anyone. I felt as if someone had pulled my heart out and stepped on it.

Besides grieving the relationship, I also missed the best friend that I had had in Nina for five years. I wished I had her to talk to about all of this. If I had only told her earlier how I felt about her, I could have avoided all this.

I decided to take a vacation and visit New York City. I wanted to forget. I needed a distraction.

KEY TAKEAWAY

Not saying anything for five years was a big mistake on my part and caused me so much pain. I could have been in a relationship with Nina earlier, and I missed the chance of great times. Who knows? Maybe I would have ended up marrying her in the end. I learned from this experience to always speak my mind, no matter how scared I am. If I feel that something is right, I will speak up. Waiting and letting fear take over will give me nothing but pain and regret.

REMEMBER...

Speaking your mind is very powerful. Never hold back and let fear take over. If you have something strong to say and you believe in it, say it!

MY JOURNEY TO THE US
HOW SMALL DECISIONS LEAD TO BIG OPPORTUNITIES

The summer was over. My breakup with Nina was tough, and I needed to get over it. I decided to take a two-week vacation to New York City with my best friend and cousin Saif. I had a cousin working at NYU as a doctor, and he lived in an apartment in the heart of downtown Manhattan close to the Empire State Building. He agreed to let us stay with him.

New York City

After a 14-hour flight, we finally arrived in New York City! What an amazing place. The lights, the streets, the skyscrapers, the thousands of tourists walking around the streets. It's fascinating and so different from Jordan.

During the day we rented bikes and were full-on tourists. At night, we hung out in the Meatpacking District, where all the bars and clubs are. We rode our bikes all around Manhattan, taking photos of everything. We toured Central Park to see where all the movies where shot. We visited the Empire State Building and Madison Square Garden. We had a great time.

New York:
Riding a bike in Central Park

New York: The fountain where
"Friends" intro video was filmed

Five days before we were to return home, I woke up to find five missed calls from my father.

I called him right away. He began the conversation with, "Hello, son. How are you?"

His tone sounded serious. "Everything is fine, Dad. I am having a good time and I will be home soon," I responded.

He asked, "What do you want to do with your life?"

What kind of question is that was the first thing that went through my mind.

It wasn't very clear to me at that time what I wanted to do with my life. I was in a phase of feeling lost and directionless.

All I knew was that I wanted to get a job in Jordan and start my engineering career. I didn't know how, when, or where. As I mentioned before, in our culture, parents usually take care of their kids financially until they can support themselves.

Other than our culture, both of my parents worked very hard, and became successful in their business ventures. They provided me with a great life and supported me financially, and I don't take that for granted. I am always very grateful for what they do for me.

After graduation I was at the point of wanting to carve my own path and support myself. I wanted to show them that I could succeed and make them proud.

My dad and I had a long conversation. The fact is, my job prospects in Jordan were limited in terms of salary as well as opportunities for a job with the potential for growth. For example, the monthly salary for an entry-level engineering job in Jordan is $500 compared with about $4,000 in the United States.

My father recommended that I stay in the US permanently and build my future there. He acknowledged that the idea of me moving to the US suddenly and leaving home would freak my mother out, but if I decided to take the step, he promised he would support me with her and help bring her around.

This phone call changed everything. I had a lot to think about.

At first, the idea didn't make sense. How could I leave my life, friends, and family in Jordan and move to America so suddenly and without any plans? It sounded insane. I had come to the US with fifteen pounds of clothes in my bag for a two-week vacation. I had no job, no friends or family. Not even a driver's license. So basically, my credit score was zero. Both of my parents have US passports, so I got citizenship when I was born, and that was a huge plus for me.

As a kid I had vacationed in several US cities but had never lived here. My whole life was in Jordan.

After a few days, a small voice in my heart told me, "Just do it." My brain was against the idea and was telling me all the reasons why I shouldn't, but as the day passed, the small whisper got louder and louder. I started to consider the idea.

"What would my life look like if I lived in the US?" I asked myself. I went online and started looking at pictures of Hollywood stars living the American dream with yachts, fancy cars, mansions, beautiful women, and private jets. It looked like a very good deal.

New York: Times Square

It is well known around the world that the United States is the land of opportunity and freedom. I started to think of my future and what kind of lifestyle I would like for my future family.

I weighed out what I would have if I stayed in Jordan versus moving to the USA:

What I personally have to succeed
Drive
Relentless optimism
I believe in my abilities and myself
I am willing to take risks
I understand what it takes to succeed
I am an engineer
Faith that everything will work out
I see endless opportunities for myself in the United States

Staying in Jordan	Moving to the USA
Friends	No friends
Family	No family
A job lined up (even though pay is low)	No job
Comfort	No experience
Connections	No promises

The hard part would be starting out with nothing. There was no company waiting with open arms to embrace me. I had no business connections. I would have to leave behind family, friends, and the comforts of home and build a completely new life.

I couldn't sleep that night. I got scared and fear hit me like a train, but something in me told me that this was the right choice, as if I had to do this for some reason. There was something pulling me toward this choice.

The most successful people in the world take big risks and make big decisions. I knew that leaving my comfort zone would be the fastest way to growth.

I'd heard a story about a successful war hero who would burn the boats of his soldiers when they reached enemy territory. He told them, "We fight or die. We are not going back home."

I ultimately made the decision to burn my personal boats and stay. I canceled my trip back to Jordan and booked a one-way ticket from New York to San Diego.

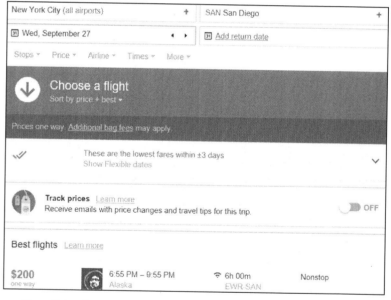

Plane ticket (I took a photo of my plane ticket and sent it to my parents).
This was September 2013.

I chose San Diego, California, because I love the beach and good weather. I'd visited San Diego as a kid and always enjoyed it.

I called my mother and told her what I had decided to do. As expected, she freaked out.

"What? Where are you going to live? How will you earn a living? Why are you leaving us?" She started to cry. I was her only child, and the idea of me leaving hit her hard.

After the initial shock, she calmed down. I told her, "Don't worry, I'll figure it out." After a long, somewhat dramatic conversation, she gave me her blessing and agreed to give me her full support in my journey.

I had one final day in New York before moving to California. I went out with my cousin and Saif to celebrate and enjoy the day downtown.

The next day I packed my bags early in the morning and took off to the airport for the six-hour nonstop flight to San Diego.

During the flight I experienced a mix of emotions—fear and excitement at the same time. It's a good thing I was naïve, because I really didn't think of the downside and the challenges that I might face. I kept daydreaming of a beautiful new life and massive success. I had absolutely no idea what was in store for me.

KEY TAKEAWAY

Tony Robbins says, "It is in your moments of decision that your destiny is shaped."

My decision to leave my old life behind and start a new one required a lot of courage and strength. I had many doubts and it was very difficult, but I just did it anyway. I had faith that everything was going to work out.

The decisions that shape our destiny aren't just the big ones; they're also the small decisions that we make every day.

For example, what I eat for dinner affects my physical destiny. A phone call to an investor could mean millions of dollars invested in my company.

I haven't always made all the right decisions, but I have made some good ones that have had a positive effect on my life.

The decisions that shape our destiny aren't just the big ones; they're also the small decisions that we make every day.

MY UNFETTERED BELIEF IN REACHING MY DREAMS

San Diego is one of the most beautiful cities in the world. It has beautiful weather year-round, beaches with amazing views, vibrant nightlife, the best companies globally in many different industries, plus friendly people everywhere. It is truly the American dream.

So the Jordanian kid arrives in San Diego. Young, ambitious, and very hungry for success.

When I called my friends and family back home and told them I'd moved to San Diego, some were supportive, while others laughed and others were negative, saying things like, "You will fail and come back to Jordan crying like a little baby."

I didn't care about any of that. All I knew was that I was going to succeed no matter what.

After doing a lot of research on the best companies in San Diego, I set my sights on one particular company.

Qualcomm.

It is one of the best tech companies in the world, and it had everything that I needed to make my engineering dreams come true.

When I talked to people about getting a job there, they told me, "It's very hard to get in and you need years of experience. Forget about it."

Challenge accepted . . .

Other people's doubts, especially coming from close friends and family, actually fueled my drive. That, and the fact that I really wanted to provide for myself with my own income and prove to my parents that I could do it.

I wanted to see what the company is all about.

Even though I was driving a rental car at that time and I had no job. I visualized myself in a Mustang convertible with two beautiful women next to me as I rode off to my amazing top-level office with an ocean view.

Qualcomm

I explored what I could of the company. I discovered they had gyms, spas, swimming pools, and even beach volleyball courts around their buildings! It was amazing!

So now the question was, "How will I get a job in Qualcomm?"

I created a beautiful vision for this new dream.

I saw myself getting accepted into my dream position, working in a top-level office with an ocean view, receiving big checks every month. Traveling the world and attending conferences.

I held this vision in my mind every day.

I started by applying online for jobs. I applied for every position on their website, even the ones that I wasn't qualified for.

I figured if they saw my name everywhere, they would take me!

But . . .

I was wrong.

Weeks and weeks passed, and I got nothing. Qualcomm is well known for being very competitive, and people said that it is nearly impossible to get in with my level of experience.

I didn't care about that. I still believed it was going to happen.

I printed out my résumé and went to the main building.

I wore a suit just as if I was going to a real interview. I was pumped up and ready. I visualized the process and myself massively succeeding.

"I don't care about money. I will work for you for free," I told the man at the front desk.

He sensed my hunger and enthusiasm. I had a great conversation with him, and he was very friendly. He actually took my résumé and forwarded it to HR.

Three weeks later . . . still no response.

I went back to him. "Hey! I still didn't hear anything back." He laughed when he saw me. I gave him another résumé and asked him to forward it again.

Again, nothing . . .

Over the next two months I drove him crazy going back and forth. But still nothing happened.

"Screw it, this is never going to work. Just go back home, you loser." This is what my mind was telling me all that time. I battled doubt and negative thoughts all the time. "I will win no matter what, and I will get that job!" is what I wrote down and read aloud every day.

I even drafted and printed out my own acceptance letter, hung it in my room, and looked at it every day as if it were real.

I decided to change my approach.

1) Network and attend events
2) Take business courses so I can be more productive with my time and make connections
3) Apply to other companies, as I need income
4) Keep visiting the Qualcomm guy

I attended three events per week, took classes at San Diego State University (SDSU), and I told every person I met about my dream of finding a job at Qualcomm and asked for their help. Showing my hunger and enthusiasm for it helped me to make good connections.

I printed out my résumé and started taking it to engineering companies all over San Diego.

I had no appointments or anything. Confidence and enthusiasm were my only assets.

After talking to more than fifty receptionists, I met one lady who really connected with me, and I felt she was the one to help me get a job.

I woke up one Sunday morning and found an email from her. I got an interview!!

The company offered me $60,000 for the first year! This offer was amazing for a fresh graduate!

To get the job, I had to pass a series of interviews, including a technical project. I prepared day and night and constantly visualized getting the job. I really believed it was going to happen.

My vision came true; the first interview was a success. I nailed four subsequent interviews. Finally only one interview remained.

I had to do a ten-day project that included complicated analysis. It was very complex.

I submitted the project, and the waiting game began. I called my family and friends and told them, "I got an engineering job! Yes! The American dream is amazing!" I already assumed that I had been accepted and made them believe it as well.

A week later I got an email from the manager telling me that the results would be posted later that evening.

I stared at the screen all day.

I started panicking, thinking, "What if I get rejected?" "All of this hard work for nothing?" My mind was all over the place. I went to take a break and grab some food. When I returned, I saw the list pop up on the screen . . .

I looked through the first page and couldn't find my name. The second page, nothing. The third, nothing. I went through all ten pages, and my name was not there. I had been rejected.

It was a very painful moment. I was angry and frustrated, and slammed the laptop shut, almost breaking it.

I called my father and ashamedly told him the story. He was supportive and told me, "You've experienced failure before. Don't let this one knock you out. Never give up, son."

He made me feel a little better, but I was knocked out for a while. I started to think about packing my bags and going home. It was tough. I was running out of time and money, too, which didn't help. Homesickness and loneliness hit me hard; it was very difficult to have no friends or people to talk to. I missed home, my friends, and family very much.

After I recovered from this down period, something in me told me to stay. I remembered my original Qualcomm vision and started to get excited again. I started to shift my thinking that I didn't get this job because I was meant to land my dream job at Qualcomm. This was just a setback until I succeeded.

My mindset began to change. Proving to my parents that I could accomplish this was also a big motivator for me.

I needed a mental boost, so I went to YouTube and searched "motivational video." I learned about Les Brown and Tony Robbins and started watching their videos.

Les Brown's quote pumped me up: "Whenever you're knocked down and land on your back, if you can look up, you can get up!"

I readjusted my plans and got back to work.

I went on a job application frenzy.

Applying for jobs online, networking, talking to people . . . you name it, I did it!

My mother came to visit me. I was crazy to the point that I actually sent her to see the receptionist at Qualcomm with my résumé in her hand. She told him, "My son is hardworking, talented, and he is willing to work for free. It is his dream to work here." He was so impressed and moved by her actions that he actually let her go in and hand the résumé to the person responsible. She got his contact information.

I called him the next day and he said, "I will talk to the people here and get back to you." A week later he called me. "I'm very sorry, Wasim. I appreciate your effort and your mother coming here, but if you want to get a position here, go get your master's degree at UCSD and come back. You don't have enough experience right now, and none of these guys want to hire you."

His words stung, but I told myself, "I don't care what this man says, I'm going to get into the company without a master's degree! Challenge accepted."

I started a new class at SDSU. In the first class the professor introduced himself and told us about his work experience.

He had actually worked at Qualcomm!!

I ran to his office after class.

He advised me to talk to recruiting and subcontracting companies, telling me that is how he got in. I was getting closer . . .

I went home and stayed up all night looking for recruiters online.

Within a month I systematically contacted fifty-five recruiters.

I called them, emailed them, went to their offices. You name it, I tried literally everything to get that job.

Hundreds of calls and many interviews resulted in rejection, but I didn't count that as a failure. It was one step closer to success.

Even when they told me, "No, I can't help," I replied, "Can you forward me to someone who can? Maybe another company perhaps?" I was ruthless.

One day the phone rang.

"Wasim, I have a financial sales job for you."

Even though it had nothing to do with what I wanted, I started to pursue it because I needed the income.

There was a five-part interview process before final acceptance. I succeeded in all of the interviews. A couple of days later I got a job offer and they were ready for me to start.

Something inside me told me not to take this job; it felt wrong.

I believed from the bottom of my heart that my destiny was to work at Qualcomm. *I should not settle for less,* I thought to myself. I called the manager and declined with an apology.

It was game time again! Qualcomm's door was very close by. I could feel it in my gut.

I went back to the hustle and tripled my efforts this time. I still got many "Nos!" but I never stopped believing that it would happen.

Two weeks later I received a phone call from recruiter number 56.

"Hello, is this Wasim?"

"Yes, it's definitely not Gregory. It's me, Wasim."

"We have reviewed your résumé and would like to set up an interview with Qualcomm for a one- to two-year contract in an entry-level position."

Oh my God! Was this a real live person or a prank call from someone?

No, it was real! It was set! My dream was coming true! I jumped all over the place and called every person on my contact list! To the haters I said, "I told you I'd do it!" To the supportive people I said, "I did it! YES! Thank you for your awesome support!"

Even though it was an entry-level position and temporary for one to two years, my game plan was to get as much experience as I could and make many connections for future opportunities. After all, this would be my first job in the US, and having a big name like Qualcomm on my résumé would benefit me massively as I moved on to other areas, so I was extremely happy for this opportunity.

I knew I still needed to pass the interviews, but I celebrated a victory as if it was already done.

The interview process was a series of seven interviews, including two technical exams. I locked myself in my room for two weeks in complete immersion of preparation. Just like a gladiator who was about to enter the arena, I was ready to die for this.

If you failed any of the interviews or tests, you were out! There were so many candidates fighting for that position. The competition was fierce.

I nailed all the interviews and just had the last interview left.

I came into the room and was pumped up and ready. The manager was nice at first, but things started to shift toward the end. He morphed into someone who didn't want me to get the job. He fired random questions at me and displayed a tough attitude.

After the meeting, I felt that I didn't do well. Negative thoughts and doubts started attacking me. "You're not going to get the job." "You failed."

I managed to shift these thoughts by again thinking of the end vision. My parents heavily supported me and lifted me up.

A week later, the phone rang . . .

"Congratulations, Wasim! You'll start your job next week!"

Woohooooooooooooooo! I felt like I'd won a million dollars! It was one of the happiest moments of my life.

All those rejections, setbacks, failures, and painful moments, and finally *this* moment came. I'd been dreaming about this moment every single day for the past six months.

I called my dad and he was beyond proud. My mother cried tears of joy.

I was now living my American dream. Finally, I had income and I was settled in San Diego. I went from no friends, no job, and no income to working at one of the best companies in the world and meeting many people who became my friends.

The day I started at Qualcomm

KEY TAKEAWAY

When I moved to the US, I started a brand-new life, but I started to visualize what my new life would look like. My vision was so clear and compelling that it excited me and gave me a bright future to look toward and work for.

I did many crazy things while applying to Qualcomm. Some worked and some didn't. If I had stuck to only one approach, it would have never worked. This is when I learned the power of trying different things to reach my goal.

Every time I made a phone call, went to meet someone, or did anything related, I always visualized myself succeeding in the process, and that boosted my confidence. Even when something didn't work out, I still held the idea of success in my mind. I also assumed success before it happened. For me, success never happened the first time I tried something, but eventually I achieved success because I never ever gave up.

It took me 20 receptionists, 55 recruiters, and 25 interviews to get the job. I knew it wasn't going to be easy, but the belief I held that it was going to happen kept me sane and moving forward. Every person that I talked to sensed that belief and confidence.

I had a very strong belief in the Law of Attraction, the vision of getting into Qualcomm, and my constant thinking of it somehow led me to that professor who had worked there. I could have picked any other class, but it's not a coincidence that things happened that way. A quote explains this perfectly: "What we think, we create. What we feel, we attract. What we imagine, we become."

I faced rejection and failure so many times. At the beginning, it hit me hard, but as I started to shift my perception into "every failed attempt is a step closer to success," it helped. I started laughing at the "Nos" that I got. I know it's so easy to perceive rejection, failures, and setbacks as a bad thing, but it ultimately made me much stronger and more resilient. I grew a strong persistence muscle.

Motivational audios from Les Brown and Tony Robbins helped me push through the difficult and painful times, so I made it a habit to listen to them daily in order to keep my mental conditioning strong.

Turning down the financial job was difficult for me because it was easy money and I really needed it, but the lesson I learned from that experience is that I should never settle for anything less than what I set out to do.

REMEMBER...

To be successful in anything you have to be relentless and keep changing your approach until it works. The secret sauce is to never give up.

FUN IN CALIFORNIA
PURSUING A GOAL INCLUDES FUN!

My journey to any goal that I set out to accomplish wasn't easy, and sometimes the stress became too much. To refresh my mind and body I always planned some time for myself where I could relax. I recognized the power of letting go: Pursuing a goal is a journey, and it's important to reap the fun and rewards along the way.

My best friend Assaf wanted to come visit, so I invited him to come so I could show him California. We planned a two-week trip throughout California and Nevada.

We started with the beaches in San Diego: Pacific Beach, Ocean Beach, Mission Beach, Del Mar Beach, Coronado. He loved all of them and especially the beautiful California girls. We went kayaking, Jet Skiing, and did different kinds of beach activities.

Las Vegas

I took him to all my favorite places, including Sea World and the San Diego Zoo. For night life, the Gas Lamp district downtown is the best place to go, because it has all the famous clubs, so we went there on the weekends. We went to see Snoop Dogg and Wiz Khalifa in a live concert and saw many DJs perform at the clubs.

Los Angeles was our next destination. We took a long drive up I-5. The freeway hugs the coast, and the views of the beach are amazing. We busted out the "California Love" song by Tupac and sang along the way. In LA, we started with Venice Beach, then hit Universal Studios and the Walk of Fame in Hollywood.

Hollywood Cool Cat

Assaf and me

If you are wondering what's up with the cat and the puppy in the photo, well, this cat is famous in Venice Beach, and all the tourists take a picture of him. He can also give you a signed picture (signed by his owner). I know it sounds crazy, but LA is cool like that. We hung out downtown in an area where all the famous clubs are, and celebrities are all over the place.

After LA, Las Vegas was our next destination. Known as Sin City, it's the most well-known party city in the world. All it has is this one strip, which you can drive through in 15 minutes, but the strip has so much action going on. There are many hotels and great restaurants.

We stayed at the Treasure Island Hotel in the middle of the strip. We walked all around the strip and checked out the hotels. Assaf took a million pictures, of course, and was amazed by the beautiful Las Vegas girls this time.

The Cirque du Soleil is one of the best shows, so we went and saw that. It was very impressive. Because it was summertime, there were many pool parties going on. We went to see DJ Tiesto perform live in a huge club called XS. The city never sleeps; people would party all night. Even at 6 a.m. you could see people leaving a club and walking the strip.

Our final destination was San Francisco. One of my closest friends from Jordan was living and studying there, so he knew where to take us. We went to see the Golden Gate Bridge, Chinatown, Union Square, Alcatraz Island, and then we went to Silicon Valley and saw the world's best tech companies: Google, HP, and many others.

After he left, I continued to plan out some vacation time at least every two months. It kept me sane and inspired to push forward without burning myself out.

Snakes in Hollywood

KEY TAKEAWAY

It is important for me to find time for fun as I am working toward my goals. I work hard and I play hard. We will spend most of our lives in the process of moving toward goals. Fun must punctuate the intensity.

It's while I'm having fun that I learn about living in the moment and enjoying it. As I go through my day, I have to remember to focus on where I am in that second and enjoy it without thinking about tomorrow, the future, or the past.

This quote explains it perfectly: "Don't wait for the perfect moment, which can be tomorrow or in the future. Take the moment you are in right now and make it perfect. Enjoy it, live it, breathe it, because life is short and will pass by your eyes if you don't enjoy every single day that you are alive."

REMEMBER...

We will spend most of our lives in the
process of moving toward goals.
Fun must punctuate the intensity.

MY DREAM OF BUSINESS
HOW TO KEEP THE FIRE BURNING FOR NEW GOALS

After my contract with Qualcomm ended, it was time for the next dream. Time for me to find a new goal. A way to achieve more personal growth.

Throughout my tenure at Qualcomm I saved money and learned about investing. I started to save a small amount of money each month and began to invest in stocks. That worked very well, and I reinvested my earnings in real estate in Jordan. We also have a small apartment in a city close to the Red Sea, and I found tenants and rented it out. These investments helped me through this transition and kept steady income coming in.

I have always been interested in business. It stems from my father having had his own business and growing up in that environment. I now had a degree and some experience in technical engineering, but no business experience.

I consulted my best friend Google again. "Best business degree?" I asked her. The MBA (master of business administration) was at the top of the list as the most prestigious. When studying for an MBA, you learn all aspects of business and you can specialize in your area of interest. My interest was innovation and entrepreneurship.

The number-one university in San Diego is UCSD (The University of California, San Diego). The business school is called the Rady School of Management. It has the number-one MBA program and is ranked among the top universities in the world. I developed the hunger to pursue the dream of getting accepted into their program.

When I consulted people, the overwhelming response I got was, "No way are you going to get in. It's very competitive, and out of the thousands of people who apply, only a handful get in." *Challenge accepted,* I thought to myself.

Each day I envisioned myself getting accepted, and I even wrote and printed out my own letter of acceptance and hung it in my room. I read it and wrote it down every day.

UNIVERSITY OF CALIFORNIA SAN DIEGO
The Rady School of Management
Summer 2015
Dear Mr. Wasim Hajjiri
Congratulations on being accepted into the MBA program at UCSD, The Rady School of Management.

My friends thought I was crazy for pursuing this goal, which appeared unattainable to many people. But I never listened to other people's limiting thinking and beliefs. I always focused on my own beliefs and on achieving massive results, and it had worked very well for me in the past. Getting into the MBA program was my next big goal. I knew it was not going to be easy. I also applied to other schools just for backup.

I researched all the MBA programs available in San Diego, checked out their ratings, and looked over their application forms. I compiled the details about each of the programs. Then I personally visited every single university. I went to admissions and told them, "I'm applying to get into the MBA program, and I need help." I compiled the names of the heads of admissions and interviewed them personally. I told them my story and asked for advice.

This gave me connections in admissions that were amazing. Everyone was very friendly and helpful. All I needed to do was to ask for help. I met one amazing lady at the Rady School of Management, Giovanna, who gave me so much guidance and inspiration it was incredible.

To be accepted, I needed to get a high grade in the infamous GRE exam, which is a test used by graduate programs and business schools. The GRE is like the SAT exam, but five times harder.

It is a four-hour hard-core exam of complex English and mathematics. My GPA in undergrad work wasn't the best, so I needed to nail this exam in order to get into any master's program. It was my only chance. I also needed to obtain a high grade in the TOEFL exam (test of English as a foreign language), because I'm an international student.

In this same period, I was also applying for jobs, as I wanted to get business experience and more income. I got an offer from an insurance company for a position in financial planning and sales. I had to pass an exam in order to get the license needed to start the job.

I had three exams to study for at the same time. Not to mention that applying to graduate school requires a lot of essays, and every application took a long time. I was determined to accomplish this next goal. By now I had learned to work hard and not stop until I reached my goal.

My life was full to the brim with the following activities:
1) Studying for the GRE exam
2) Studying for the TOEFL exam
3) Studying for the financial license exam
4) Writing essays
5) Filling in applications
6) Networking
7) Meeting with admissions
8) Research
9) Exercising
10) Meditating
11) Relaxing

Re-lated items	Main goal	Date (dead-line)	Action plan	Purpose of the goal	Vision
9,10,11	To be in top physical and mental shape	Daily	1. Hit the gym for 1 hour in the morning 2. Meditate for 10 minutes upon waking up 3. Relax 1–2 hours at night, not doing anything	I want to be strong to tackle my goals and succeed without burning out	Succeeding in the action items with high energy and determination
1,2,4, 5,7,8	Get accepted into the MBA program at UCSD	Summer 2015	1. Write essays for 1 hour twice a week 2. Study for the GRE exam for 4 hours daily 3. Study for the TOEFL exam for 1 hour daily 4. Study for the license exam for 1 hour daily 5. Keep contacting admissions if I have any questions 6. Finish all applications 7. Research interview questions, exam questions, etc. . . . 1 hour per week	I want to obtain the best business knowledge to start a successful business. I want to make new friends, meet people, and make my parents proud	Getting an acceptance letter
3,6	Get accepted into a great position	March 2015	Study license exam 2 hours per day Attend 1 networking event per week	Income Business experience	Acing the test and starting the job

I used the same technique of goal setting that I mentioned in previous chapters. But this time I added a row (related items) to add all of the action items that relate into one main goal. This way I would focus on three outcomes instead of twelve action steps.

To add to the mix, during this time my father got sick. Being thousands of miles away from him was hard. I really wished I could be in Jordan with him, but I couldn't leave because I had all these exams coming up. Every time I called him, he told me, "I'm so proud of you, son! Don't worry about me. Go after your dreams. I will be just fine."

I developed an obsession to succeed and make him proud. I set a daily plan to study for 8–10 hours and spend 2–4 hours writing essays and filling in applications. The time I spent at the gym was my only rest period in the day. Lifting weights helped to keep my mind focused. During this time, my relationship with my girlfriend suffered as I didn't have time to see her, and that was more drama for me to deal with.

My mother was traveling back and forth between Jordan and San Diego. She is always my number-one cheerleader. I was so fortunate to have the support of both my parents on my journey.

I was completely stressed out, and there were many times I doubted my ability to succeed and considered giving up. But buried deep down in my soul was a fire burning to make my parents proud. This kept me going and helped me push through the tough times.

After months and countless restless nights of preparation, the day came for the ultimate battle: the GRE exam.

It is four hours of mayhem. You have 30 seconds to answer each question or you won't finish the exam. Bathroom breaks are out of the question. I didn't drink water to avoid having to take time out to run to the bathroom. Besides being stressed, I was hungry and thirsty the whole four hours.

The time passed in a blur. I worked hard and gave it my absolute best. By the end, I felt like Frodo must have when the ring finally made it into the fire at the end of the movie *The Lord of the Rings*. Now I had to wait for my results. I kept visualizing getting the acceptance letter and living the student life.

A week later I got the test results, and I had achieved the grade that would get me into graduate school. I was so happy. I immediately called my dad. The news lifted his spirits!

Now I had to wait for actual acceptance from UCSD, the Rady School of Management. Tick tock. Time felt frozen. Self-doubt always tends to creep in somehow at these difficult times, but I fought the doubt constantly by believing that I would be accepted. Every single morning, noon, and night I visualized the end goal. "Yes! It will happen!" "Yes, I am accepted." I chanted these phrases in my head thousands of times. I stayed in touch with Giovanna; she kept me motivated and gave me a huge boost of confidence.

It was a beautiful summer day—a Monday, to be exact. I woke up and did my usual routine. Then I opened my email and found a bright red dot in my inbox. The sender was "UCSD, The Rady School of Management."

My destiny was waiting for me right there. I stared at the red dot for ten minutes feeling as if my heart was going to explode. Sweat started dropping from my forehead. "Should I open it now or later?" I questioned. Finally, I summoned the courage to open it.

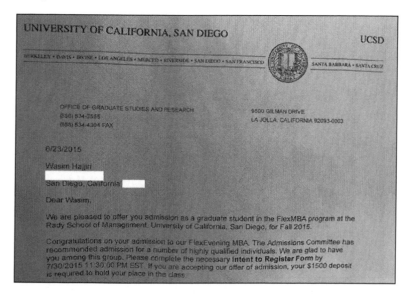

"We are pleased to offer you admission as a graduate student in the FlexMBA program at the Rady School of Management, University of California, San Diego, for Fall 2015."

Yes! Woohooo! Success! Glory! Victory! Hoooooraaaaayyyyyyyy!

Thank you, God, for this opportunity!

This acceptance felt better than winning the lottery. I was ecstatic and went crazy, jumping all over the room with laughter and total joy. It was an amazing celebration. I called my father.

"Hello, Dad."

"Yes, son?"

"I GOT IN!"

He started laughing and said, "I told you you would succeed!"

KEY TAKEAWAY

Using different strategies allowed me to deal with many different things at once. The strong belief that everything was going to work out helped me push through doubt, fear, and negative self-talk. Exercising and eating healthy daily kept me energized and alleviated the stress.

REMEMBER...

A strong belief that everything is going to work out will help you push through doubt, fear, and negative self-talk.

MY FATHER'S PASSING
FINDING STRENGTH IN SORROW

had been accepted into the MBA program in one of the best universities in the world and I had just started a new job with an insurance company. Everything seemed on track, and I was looking forward to getting started in this new phase of my life. Then my father got very sick again. As his health declined, the pessimism in the family grew. My mother was the only one unaffected by fear and pessimism. She clung to hope and did her best to give me hope as well.

I found it hard to be positive. I was full of questions and emotions. I felt very angry and frustrated. Why was this happening to my father? I went to a very dark place and felt completely down.

Weeks later I got a call to come home immediately. I quit my new job so I could return to Jordan to spend time with and focus on my father. My new job suddenly paled in comparison to taking care of my father.

The 24-hour journey from San Diego to Jordan felt like a nightmare. There was nowhere I could run to or hide from the thoughts flying around in my head.

What if my father dies? What will I do? What will happen to my mom? What is going to happen to our family? Many negative thoughts bombarded me.

I tried to talk some sense into myself. "You're making all of this up. Toughen up, Wasim! It's going to be okay." I started to shift my focus to my dad getting better and living. I was going to go back and do my best to lift him up and give him hope so that he could keep on living.

I took sleeping pills on the plane so that I could sleep instead of worry. Finally the plane arrived. On the taxi ride home, I started to plan how I would deal with everything coming at me. Not only supporting my father personally but also dealing with the rest of the family. My main strategy was to stay positive no matter what happened.

I arrived at my house not knowing what to expect. As soon as I opened the door, my dad was there. He had a big smile and laughed. He was so happy to see me. He was very weak and had lost so much weight. I was heartbroken to see him like this, but I held myself together and showed nothing but a big smile.

The moment I saw my father

Seeing me boosted his spirit. The first thing he said to me was, "Son, I am so proud of all you have accomplished. I know my time is limited and I might die soon, but I will die happy, knowing that my youngest son is working hard and achieving big things in life. I know you will always make me proud. Even when I'm in my grave I will be cheering and rooting for you from the bottom of my heart."

His speech froze me for a minute. I hugged him again and cried.

We talked day and night for the next three weeks. He was weak, but with the little energy he had, he managed to give me a smile here and there. I kept encouraging him to live and not give up. The atmosphere around me was very emotional, pessimistic, and dramatic as my sisters, aunts, and family members constantly cried when they saw him. I had to fight all of that and somehow stay positive.

I kept joking with my dad about finding him a new young and beautiful wife. He would crack up and laugh. Seeing him so weak and sick was tearing my heart out, but my only focus was for him to get better and live.

With the little energy he had, Dad gave me a smile for the photo

I stayed in Jordan for three weeks while Dad's health stabilized. I was still concerned about his health overall, but the MBA program was about to start. With my dad improving and with his encouragement, I returned to San Diego to start the program.

On a normal Saturday morning, I went to the boxing gym for an hour. I left my phone in the car. When I came back, I saw six missed calls from a Jordanian number I didn't recognize. I tried calling back, but no one answered. Then I got a text message from my brother telling me to call him right away.

I called him. He paused before speaking. "Where are you?" he asked me.

"I'm sitting in my car," I responded.

"I am so sorry, Wasim. Our father passed away this morning."

A million questions came to mind. "What?" "How?" "What happened?" I tensed up and started panicking. I'll never forget the feeling that I was hit with. It was like a bullet entered my chest through my heart and got stuck in the middle. I felt like my whole world collapsed over my head.

I sat in my car in shock for thirty minutes. Finally, I thought to call my best friend and roommate, Assaf. He had known my father and had a great relationship with him. We cried together. When the call was over, I felt calm enough to start driving back to my house. I opened all the car windows so that I could get some fresh air.

As I got closer to my house, I became overwhelmed with emotions of grief, anger, sadness. When I pulled up to the house, Assaf was standing outside waiting for me. He ran to the car and hugged me.

I started screaming, "This is not fair!" "Why did this happen!" "Why?!" "Why me!?" and burst into tears.

I was surprised to see my girlfriend and two other friends at my house. Assaf had called them, and they came right away to be there for me. My girlfriend stayed with me for the next few days and helped me through the grief. It was a terrible time, but it felt good to be supported. I cannot imagine how I would have gotten through on my own.

The next ten days were some of the more difficult ones of my life. But slowly I came out of that dark place of grief.

I remember having dreams that were full of happy memories of my father. I dreamed about him being alive and healthy, my childhood on our farm, and I saw him playing basketball with me in the yard and walking around with our dogs having a great time.

I believe that God gave me these dreams to help me get through this rough time.

Slowly I started to get better, and I built a new belief that I would carry my father with me wherever I go.

My mother was suffering through her own grief, but we were able to have moments of conversation that were very soothing. She told me, "Son, we will get through this together. Your father died very proud of you, and he is in a better place. He was sick and suffering. Heaven is a better place for him."

As I lay there one day in my bedroom with my head under the pillow, I heard my father's voice asking me, "Wasim, what is your dream? You can achieve big things. I believe in you; make me proud."

I started to visualize my father in front of me talking to me. The first day of class was coming up soon. I didn't have much time. I decided to get back up and fight. I will do this for him. I will never give up.

Soon I was standing at the front gate of the Rady School of Management, UCSD. My business journey had begun!

The Rady School of Management is well known for entrepreneurship and innovation. More than 100 companies have formed from the prestigious Rady incubator program called the StartR accelerator. My passion is to learn business so that I can start my own company just like my father. I made it one of my goals to enter StartR. At that time I also decided to write this book and dedicate it to him. I never knew that I had a hidden passion for writing, but the pain somehow unleashed that power within me and writing helped me mentally.

I took this picture and sent it to my mother while I was going to my first class

The students in my cohort were amazing—all from different countries, backgrounds, and industries. I loved the diversity. I started building relationships with them, and I felt like they were my new family. Participation made up a big percentage of the grades in classes, so everyone was pushed to speak up in class. The atmosphere was very uplifting as everyone supported each other. As I went through many difficult nights, this new experience and writing this book kept me busy and helped keep my mind off my father's passing.

The classes were very hands-on and practical, unlike the usual "study this book and take a test" type of experience. We did projects and presentations based on real business situations, and everyone learned the tools necessary to excel in their industries.

My new Rady family

The classes were very challenging and the workload was heavy. But I worked very hard and gave my all to each presentation, assignment, and project. I didn't focus too much on grades, but I wanted to absorb all the material so I could apply it later when I started my business.

The curriculum was designed to be 50% core classes and 50% electives, so you could choose all the classes that you were interested in. I chose classes that related to entrepreneurship and innovation. I learned about how to run a successful business.

Each professor had extensive experience, and all were very kind and friendly. Throughout the courses I formed good relationships with them.

I attended seminars in which the school brought in successful CEOs from the world's best companies. We heard them speak and learned from their experience.

I also attended entrepreneurship events in which students pitched business ideas to investors and battled in competitions to raise money for their company. The companies that the students formed were wildly successful, and most of them are young. I was really amazed by this environment, and I got inspired to unleash my creativity and start my own business which included my book.

Our dean, Robert Sullivan, was involved in these events. He is so passionate about the business school and the students. I interacted with him one on one several times, and he helped me develop my ideas and always inspired me to move forward. When I told him about this book, he was very supportive and said it aligns with his vision of Rady students changing the world.

Robert Sullivan, Dean of the Rady School of Management

Through the Rady network and our amazing career coach Linda Kurtz I got in touch with my publishing coach, Bethany Kelly, who is the reason this book turned from a dream into reality.

During my last year in the MBA program, I had an idea to create a service product.

I figured that I had learned so much through my experience of getting into Qualcomm, I wanted to create a program that will help other people get their dream job.

That is when Bethany introduced me to another amazing mentor, Liz Goodgold. She helped me put my ideas together and start the process, and thanks to her I now have an online course that helps students and young professionals get their dream job.

As we were approaching graduation, our final project was called Lab to Market. In this project, we develop a business idea fully. We start with research and end with running it in the actual market. During that course my two friends Josh Shaffer and Immad Ajjawi had already started a company called Globier, which is the world's first glow-in-the-dark beer. It was in the initial stages, and since my business idea wasn't fully developed, I joined their team. I learned so much while the business grew to the big success it is today.

While doing presentations and taking communication classes, I discovered that I have a passion for speaking. The products, speaking, and book became my idea to apply for the StartR program, so I could start moving forward in making my business a big success.

Thirty-five teams applied to the program, and only six teams would be picked.

To get into the program, there were two phases. The first phase was to fill out an online application, which was long, as it outlined all the details of the business. After submitting the application, the thirty-five teams are narrowed down to ten teams.

Phase two included a business idea pitch in front of a panel of judges which included them asking questions, just like pitching to investors. Then the ten teams are narrowed down to six.

I was competing against students with master's degrees and PhDs, with biomedical ideas, engineering ideas, technology ideas. All kinds of unique innovation. It was very competitive. I worked very hard on the application and made sure to stand out.

Just as I did before, I visualized getting accepted into the program every day. I made it through the first phase.

I practiced my speech for the pitch for a whole week, day in and day out. I knew the material like the back of my hand.

Then I was standing in front of the panel and speaking with all my heart and soul. As I spoke, I wasn't getting the reaction I'd expected from the judges. Everyone looked very serious. After I finished, they asked me questions and I answered all of them. Their reaction left me with feelings of doubt and negative self-talk. But I still believed that I would get into the program.

A week later I got the news that I had been accepted! It was an amazing celebration for me, as I was approaching graduation at that time.

The program provided me with mentorship, networking opportunities, investment opportunities, cash prizes from competitions, and really took my business from an idea to a huge success.

With Herb

StartR connected me with Herb Meistrich, who is by far one of the most incredible people that I met. He became a phenomenal mentor and allowed me to grow not just in my business but in other areas of life as well due to his incredible experience and genuine kindness.

"The Rady School of Management develops ethical and entrepreneurial leaders who make a positive impact in the world through innovation, collaboration and knowledge."

This is the mission statement of the school. The founder, Ernest Rady, donated $100 million to the school in 2015 to make sure his legacy lives on through its students. He believes that every one of us will succeed and change the world.

KEY TAKEAWAY

At some point or another, we all have to deal with very difficult situations, and I understand that some situations are harder on certain people than others.

When I was faced with my father passing, I experienced all the negative emotions you can imagine: anger, bitterness, frustration. I could have stayed in those emotions for a long time. I could have stayed depressed and crying in bed, but I did things that helped me get over it. 1) I found an empowering meaning from the experience. I decided that I wanted to accomplish my next dream for my father and make him proud up there in heaven. This lit a fire in my soul and inspired me. 2) I remained around other people as much as I could, even when I didn't feel like it. My friends helped lift me out of the depressed phase and get better. 3) I found something new to spend my time on (I stayed as active as I could). 4) I exercised a lot. It really helped me deal with the sadness.

REMEMBER...

The loss of my father was very hard, but
I managed to find an empowering meaning.
That pain drove me to write this book.

13

THE ULTIMATE TRAINING CAMP
DISCOVERING UNWAVERING COMMITMENT

As a child, I watched athletes like Kobe Bryant play basketball on TV. I loved sports in general and I wanted to excel, but I never found a sport that worked for me. I swam and played basketball and soccer, but never excelled to the point that I could compete professionally. It was a dream for me to become a professional competitive athlete, but it didn't help that I was chubby, short, and out of shape.

At 17, I joined a fitness club close to my house. I started out with boxing. I enjoyed it, and over four months, I lost a lot of weight.

I was happy with my progress. But I wanted to get bigger, stronger, and gain muscle mass. So I started lifting weights. From the second I held my first dumbbell, I fell in love with weight lifting. From that point on, I trained six times a week.

As the months passed, I started to get stronger and better. I wasn't the chubby short kid anymore.

For the first three years of my training I mostly trained on my own, with a part-time coach on the side. Then I wanted to up my game. Abbadi was in his fifties and a well-known coach in Jordan. A weight-lifting champion himself, he also trained many athletes who became world champions. He is very serious about training and has helped people transform themselves mentally and physically.

Abbadi and me

I set up a meeting with him the following week and signed him on as my coach. His gym was small and had only the basic equipment. No TVs. No air conditioning. Only fans. However, he had built a great family community at his gym based on commitment and respect. Everyone knew he was very serious about training and respected him for it. It was a hard-core gym.

Training started on the first day. He had strict rules that everybody had to follow: (1) no cellphones, (2) no headphones, (3) no talking or fooling around or wasting time. We were only there to focus on weight lifting and training hard. I felt like I had just enrolled in the army. If you didn't like the rules or were unwilling to follow them, you simply got kicked out. "No pain, no gain" was his motto.

He had around 50 members in the gym, and he was the personal trainer for each one. He remembered each member's name and exactly where they were in their training. He knew what they had done yesterday and what they were going to do tomorrow. He was very sharp. People who trained with Abbadi never went to another gym. His competitive advantage was his personality and the fact that he was an inspiration to young people.

He put me on a strict diet. "Where does McDonald's fit into this diet?" I asked him. He laughed and said, "No more McDonald's if you want to take it to the next level."

Every day he made me push through my limits in each set, each repetition. "Come on!" "You can do it!" "One last rep!" "You want to be a champion, don't you?" "Never give up!" I felt like I was dying most of the time, but he motivated me to continue. When every muscle in my body told me that I was incapable of doing one more rep, he pushed me to do five more!

I would wake up the day after training so sore that I could barely get my body out of bed.

Abbadi enforced the fact that we absolutely could not skip training for any reason. Unless we were deathly ill or facing a family emergency, we had better show up at the gym. People who skipped too much training were kicked out. Not nicely. Commitment and dedication were a must.

There were plenty of days when I didn't feel like going to the gym or was too tired. But one phone call with Abbadi had me running to the gym.

Over the months, I developed a very strong habit of training. I couldn't skip any day, and I if I had to for some reason, I felt depressed.

Abbadi is the one who planted the seed in my head that I might be able to compete professionally in the future, though he told me it would take dedication and years of training.

After getting to know him well, I asked him about his missing fingers. He was missing two and a half fingers on one hand. He told me he lost them in a horrific car accident in which he almost lost his life. This accident happened just before a competition. After he recovered, he continued to train with his arm wrapped up and later won the competition. I was continually amazed at the level of dedication he had toward fitness and the people he trained in his gym.

I trained with him nonstop for four years. During that time I experienced a complete physical transformation, gaining muscle mass and getting leaner. I never expected to stop working with him, but my trip to New York changed everything.

When I called Abbadi from New York and told him that I wasn't returning to Jordan, he was devastated. He was one of my best mentors and was just like a brother to me.

It was also very hard for me to move on and not train with him anymore. I remain in contact with him to this day. Every time I visit Jordan I go see him, and he is very proud of my accomplishments.

KEY TAKEAWAY

Abbadi was a great mentor and he influenced my life in a positive way, but he was a different sort of mentor as he was very strict and his rules were hard-core. The journey with him was challenging, but what he taught me helped me become a better person, athlete, and bodybuilder.

When Abbadi pushed me past my limits, it made me physically and mentally stronger. It unleashed a powerful part of my personality that I discovered. It taught me to push through the uncomfortable feeling that I get when I want to do something and I don't feel like it.

You might experience a type of mentor like Abbadi. One who pushes you further than you feel ready to go. From my experience, the more hard-core the mentor is, the further you will push yourself and the better you will perform.

I believe we all need to push through our thresholds and that uncomfortable feeling if we want to accomplish something great. A great quote that I like states, "If it was easy, everyone would do it."

Abbadi used to tell me that the difference between a champion and an average athlete is their ability to push through the hard, uncomfortable times over and over, every day, and still win.

REMEMBER...

The more hard-core the mentor is, the further you will push yourself and the better you will perform.

JUST LIKE ARNOLD SCHWARZENEGGER
DOING WHAT IT TAKES TO WIN

always idolized Arnold Schwarzenegger. I had a crazy dream of standing on a competition stage holding gold medals and first-place trophies over my head as people cheered for me. Arnold was a twelve-time world champion, famous actor, and more recently a politician. His work ethic and dedication inspired me to achieve big things.

Arnold weighed around 245 pounds while competing. I, on the other hand, weighed 170, so Arnold's weight was out of reach for me. Another person that I idolized was Frank Zane. Frank Zane was also a multiple world champion, and he was famous for having one of the most symmetrical and aesthetic physiques in the history of the sport.

He weighed around 190 pounds and is one of the very few people who beat Arnold. Ideally, I wanted my physique to be like his, as I was always interested in the aesthetic look.

One day at work I told my co-worker, Eric, about this crazy vision that I had. Eric happened to know a coach who prepares athletes for competitions. He was one of the best in San Diego.

Eric introduced me to Jeff Kotterman and his TriSystem gym. From him I learned about the INBA (International Natural Bodybuilding Association). They use the WADA (World Anti-Doping Agency) system to ensure that athletes are natural and don't use any drugs or stimulants (this is the same agency that they use at the Olympics for drug testing). I found exactly what I wanted. The INBA is the largest natural fitness organization in the world.

The division that I was interested in competing in is called "Physique." Individuals who compete in this division focus on being lean, muscular, and symmetrical. The average weight class is 150–170 pounds.

It was September, and my first championship match was two months away. I officially joined Jeff's team, TriSystem, and began to train. The diet was insane. The food is weighed by ounces, fruits by pieces, and salads by the cup. I dropped from 13% body fat to 8%. Training spanned 2–4 hours daily and included heavy weight lifting and cardio.

13% ⟶ 8%

My transformation

When you're eating low calories, the mind starts to play tricks on you. You know how pregnant women crave certain foods? That's how I was. I craved chocolate all the time.

Posing is a skill that must be learned in order to succeed on stage in the competition. It's the way you compete against other athletes and show off the best of your physique. It's very strategic. You can use posing to hide your body's weak points and elevate the strong ones. The competition also includes an individual routine, so the judges can focus and judge each athlete individually. This routine is also an opportunity for us to show the artistic side of posing and gain more points on the score card. Jeff's team included two other guys, David and John, who helped me with posing. I felt very awkward at first and didn't know what I was doing, but after months of practice I started to get better. I visualized myself winning every single day. I had a strong belief that I would get to the top, no matter what. Even though many days I didn't feel like training, I pushed myself to go to the gym and finish the workout despite the negative self-talk and my brain telling me, "Stay home and rest. Why go to the gym?"

I watched videos of Arnold and Frank Zane training, giving speeches, and the famous documentary "Pumping Iron" many times to get inspired and learn their psychology and philosophy of training. They were always laser-sharp focused and had tunnel vision. When Arnold trained biceps, for example, that was his only thought while in the gym. He would visualize the muscle growing and would train accordingly. Frank Zane's and Arnold's training methods were unique and very different from other athletes. That's what gave them the edge.

Many times as I trained in the gym I would listen to their motivational videos, and their voice alone would pump me up and make me push myself to the limit.

Finally, the day of my first competition arrived! It felt just like a dream. I had watched Arnold compete since I was a kid, and now I was the one who would be on stage! I was crazy excited. I felt like a world champion even before I stepped on that stage. I had only one thought that day: "Win first place no matter what."

To get the muscles pumped up and ready for stage, all the athletes went backstage to lift weights and do a light exercise routine.

When I saw how conditioned the other athletes were, I started to panic and negative self-talk hit. "You're not good enough." "These other people are better than you." "Why are you even here?"

Although I was very confident and I had strong beliefs that I was going to win, my emotions started to turn on me.

To change that state, I walked outside the auditorium and took in some fresh air, I started to think about my father and why I was doing all this. I wanted to make him proud, and I wasn't going to let the pressure get to me. I put on some motivational music and started saying positive affirmations to myself. Slowly, I calmed down and regained some confidence. I went back inside and got in complete focus mode.

To become the champion, I had to beat twelve other competitors in my category.

It was showtime!

I step on stage, visualizing myself as a gladiator going to the arena. Thirteen warriors battling it out for the first-place prize. Years and years of training have been put into sculpting these physiques. No one was going out easy, and there was no mercy.

I tried my best and posed my heart out. With sweat pouring down my chest, I smile and look at the crowd. I hear cheering from my friends, which gives me a good boost.

After prejudging, there is a break until the night show. By this time all the scores have been decided and the judges know who got first place.

After a whole day of competing, during which I had to work very hard to keep myself in the right mindset, I lined up on stage with the other twelve athletes to hear the results. The placing started. "And the thirteenth place goes to . . . Wasim Hajjiri!"

I felt like someone had punched me in the face, I came in LAST! I felt completely humiliated, and all I wanted to do was get off the stage. I held myself in place and smiled the best I could while all twelve other placements were announced.

My close friends and girlfriend were with me. They took me out for a nice cheat meal to get my mind off my loss. When I went back home, I made a promise to myself to take the competitions more seriously. I told myself I would never quit until I got the gold medal. I would make my father proud. My belief was, "Even if I lose ten competitions, I'm going to win number eleven."

I called my mother, as she was in Jordan at that time. She lifted my spirits. She told me, "Your father would have been proud of you, and I am even more proud of you." I'm so blessed to have a mother like her.

I told Jeff to triple the intensity of the diet and workouts. I told him my dream of winning the Olympia and that I was willing to do whatever it took to get there.

I went crazy at the gym and redoubled my efforts. I talked to some of the judges after the competition to see what I needed to work on in the off season, and they gave me good feedback. Jeff and I built my training plan based on their input. I started lifting heavy weights in my weaker muscle groups, and week by week I noticed improvements.

KEY TAKEAWAY

When I got into sports, I found that it is just like life and business. Without a strong belief in winning, I might fall from the first fail. My belief going into the competitions was that I was going to win just like Arnold and hold the trophies above my head.

Even though I lost, it was the belief that made me commit to the training and put my heart into it. My father's passing acted as an inspiration for me, and that helped pump me up daily.

REMEMBER...

Without a strong belief in winning,
you might fall from the first fail.

15

SEEING ARNOLD
AND FRANK ZANE LIVE
SURROUND YOURSELF WITH
THE RIGHT PEOPLE

During my competition training, I went to a big fitness event called the LA Fitness Exposition. I heard that Arnold and Frank Zane sometimes show up there, and being a crazy fan, I wanted to meet both of them. I met famous athletes and champions like Dexter Jackson and Jay Cutler, but Arnold and Frank didn't show up. I met many other people who competed, and they gave me great advice.

Dexter Jackson

Jay Cutler

I met a man called Eric the Trainer who actually trained Arnold's son. He is a host of a TV show called *Celebrity Sweat*, and he owns a private gym in LA where he trains Hollywood celebrities. He also knew Frank Zane and told me that he lived in San Diego and that I should go see him and tell him that he sent me. Eric gave me amazing words of encouragement and told me to attend an event called the Arnold Classic, as Arnold attends it every year. I was amazed by this coincidence. My vision was to meet Arnold and Frank, and then I meet this guy who knows both of them.

Eric the Trainer

I left the LA Fitness event inspired and with a new group of friends who all had the same mindset of competing and winning. We stayed in contact and kept encouraging each other to push forward and train hard.

Two months later I found myself in Columbus, Ohio, at the Arnold Classic. My friend Assaf came with me. Two hundred and twenty thousand people from all over the world come to this event. It includes all sports, not just bodybuilding.

All the famous bodybuilders were there. I had to wait in line hours to meet some of them. There was even a long line to take a picture with the Arnold statue. I met "The Mountain," the actor from the *Game of Thrones* series. He wanted to break a world powerlifting record of 1,000 pounds. He is 6'9" (2.1 meters) and weighs 400 pounds (182 kilos).

The Mountain

I saw that C.T. Fletcher had a booth. He's famous for his documentary on Netflix, *My Magnificent Obsession,* which is the inspirational story of how he became a six-time world weightlifting champion. The line for meeting him was two hours long, so I skipped it.

The famous Arnold statue

Then I saw Eric the Trainer, who knew C.T. He took us right to him; we skipped the line and talked to him. I thought to myself, *Wow, am I in a movie?*

In the middle of the event, they announced that Arnold was there. I didn't meet him but saw him speaking live, which was a dream come true.

Being in that atmosphere around these champions and amazing people shifted my mindset and made me think even broader and bigger. When I went back home I decided to stay around this kind of vibe.

David and John, who were part of team TriSystem, were professionals who had won many gold medals and awards. I started to train with them. Initially it felt awkward, as I was in the amateur ranks with only one competition under my belt (in which I got last place), but I pushed myself to get better so that I could reach their level. That raised the intensity of my training and kept me on the edge.

"Who you surround yourself with is who you become, and proximity is power," Tony Robbins says in his speeches. I learned that surrounding myself with people who are very successful had a direct impact on my own success and it lifted me higher and pushed me to the next level.

(L-R) Assaf, C.T., Eric the Trainer, me   Arnold interviewing Kai Greene

KEY TAKEAWAY

Going to the fitness expos had a powerful impact on my psychology, training, and overall attitude. I found new mentors like Eric the Trainer. Because of his high level of success, I valued his feedback. Him telling me that I had potential for success inspired me and made the idea of achieving my dreams even bigger. Training with people at a higher level also pushed me to up my game and stay on the edge.

REMEMBER...

Who you surround yourself with is who you become. I decided to hang around people who are successful, and that allowed me to up my game and stay on the edge.

LOSING TO WIN
THE NEED FOR FAILURE TO ACHIEVE SUCCESS

came in seventh place in my second championship in Bakersfield, California. I wasn't satisfied. First place was the goal, and I wasn't going to stop.

During that time, I was working, going through the master's program, and competing at the same time, so I decided to take a mini vacation. My girlfriend and I decided to go to Hawaii. We spent five days in Maui. I had never been there and it had always been on my bucket list.

Bakersfield Championship, March 2016

We rented a car and drove all over the island. Clear skies, tropical weather, amazing beaches, and the sound of birds everywhere. It was a beautiful experience. We hiked through the mountains and saw many waterfalls and volcanoes.

Because I was preparing for my third competition, I stuck with my diet, so I cooked and prepared all my meals during the trip. Even when we went for hikes and jumped in the waterfalls, when it was time for my meal, I would pull out my Tupperware container and eat my food. People would look at me and think I was crazy. I was dedicated to the diet and wasn't going to take a break under any circumstances.

Maui, Hawaii

Maui, Hawaii

My third championship was held in Corona, California. I got fourth place. Ouch. I was getting closer, but still wasn't there. It hurt to come in fourth, but I still wasn't going to stop.

Before the next competition, I decided to go visit Eric the Trainer to get some inspiration. I went to his private gym in Hollywood where he trains all the celebrities. It had brand-new equipment, a boxing ring, outside gym, and everything was custom-made for his gym. In his office, he had pictures signed from all the body-building legends, actors, athletes, stars, and even Muhammad Ali.

Corona Championship 2016

We did a workout and he gave me some new insights and tips. Tyler Williams, who is a famous actor, walked in during our workout! It was surreal. I had watched Tyler act in *Everybody Hates Chris* and *The Walking Dead,* and now he was right in front of me! Shortly after that, one of the actors from *The Fast and the Furious* walked in as well. I thought I was in a dream. I talked to them and told them about my upcoming competition, and they gave me a huge push. I felt the genuineness and humbleness from them, and it was an amazing experience.

119

Tyler Williams

Eric's office with signed
pictures from legends

An actor from
The Fast and the Furious

Hyde from the series
That '70s Show

Eric told me to go see Frank Zane in person, because he lived
in San Diego and owned a private gym in which he trains people.
That news blew my mind! As soon as I got back to San Diego, I
did some research and found out where he was. I spoke to him
on the phone the first time, and it was just like a dream.

I found all of his information on his website, www.frankzane.com.

I was about to go see one my idols, and what's funny is that
he lived ten minutes away from me. His gym looked like a
historic museum. It was filled with photos of him competing

all the way back to the 1960s and 1970s. He was very friendly and warm from the instant I spoke to him. He told me stories about the golden era of bodybuilding and how he used to hang out with Arnold and all the famous bodybuilders who became legends. It was surreal.

He even went to the first Mr. Olympia competition (which is basically the Olympics of bodybuilding) in 1965 and watched Larry Scott win. He is 75 years old and has been involved in the sport since the age of 15.

The legendary Frank Zane!!

Of course while talking to him, I told him how much I had idolized him since I was a kid. He sensed my enthusiasm and was kind enough to actually give me some gifts.

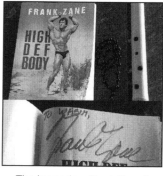

The legendary Frank Zane!!   The legendary Frank Zane!!

A signed book, a flute that he hand-made, and a good-luck-blessing stone bracelet.

This meant the world to me. Frank Zane is known world-wide as being the best and most artistic poser in the history of bodybuilding. He taught me a new posing routine and gave me a new nutrition and training regimen.

"You have a great physique and will excel in the sport" were his words to me. I literally wrote them down.

I left his gym feeling like a million bucks! I was inspired and more excited about training than I've ever been!

I competed in the Arizona Championships and got second place. I could smell victory, I was so close. I also started competing in a new division called Sports and Fitness Model, which was similar to Physique, plus it involved a speech. Because I love speaking, this was my chance to share my story to inspire and pump up the audience.

After that, I had four months to prepare for the Team USA nationals, which is a big deal, and I was very excited to be competing on a national level. My mother would be coming to attend this event. It pumped me up to train harder and added a massive element of stress. I couldn't lose in front of my mom. She was counting on me to win!

Arizona Championships 2016

That whole summer I focused on training, speaking, and nothing else. I was obsessed with winning. Day and night I visualized getting on that stage and receiving the gold medal.

My mother and friends worried about me, as I didn't see them too much. At that point, barbells and dumbbells were my best friends.

I kept watching motivational videos and read about body-building to learn new things that would give me an advantage.

I went into the competition with complete focus and deter-mination. I had reached the peak with my physique, and I lit-erally gave it everything that I had in the training camp. My speech was solid as well. It outlined my journey coming from Jordan, my mother, and my journey with fitness while my father passed away.

After a long, tough battle, I finally heard the words that I had been waiting to hear . . .

"And the first-place gold medal goes to . . . Wasim Hajjiri!"

I won! Wow! It was one of the best feelings I've ever had! All my hard work and failures finally paid off. I felt beyond joy, excitement, and happiness. I felt like more than a million bucks! My dreams were finally coming true!

Team USA Nationals Gold Medal, 2016

The best part of my win was that my mom was there. She has been my number-one fan ever since I was very young. She always believed in me and my dreams and pushed me to win. Whether it was school or sports, she always cheered me on. As soon as they announced my name as the first-place winner, I looked at her face and she was screaming her heart out with tears of joy. It was amazing. I ran off the stage and hugged her.

Ever since my father passed away, I felt that I had the full responsibility of taking care of her, and part of that was to make her proud. This fueled my passion to be successful in anything that I set out to do.

I called everyone I knew in Jordan to tell them about the news because it was such a big deal. My friends, cousins, family, their friends, everyone you can imagine. I blasted the news all over social media. I got so many phone calls of people congratulating me. It was amazing to see that some people were more excited than I was!

Now I finally qualified to compete at the Natural Olympia, which was six weeks away and the most competitive of them all. It is considered the Olympics of natural bodybuilding and fitness.

KEY TAKEAWAY

I went from last place to first place! That first time I lost was tough, but it lit a fire in my soul and made me obsessed with winning, and I kept working until my dream became a reality.

What I learned from this journey of winning the Team USA nationals is that failure is necessary for success. Any big goal that I have will not come easy, and there will be many bumps along the way. It taught me to aim even higher and go for bigger goals. Dealing with failure made me stronger and more resilient.

Holding on to the vision of success is key to keeping the drive going as well. Meeting Frank Zane also gave me a huge push, and I felt that winning would make him proud as well. I talked about the importance of mentors before, but I learned it is a never-ending process of gaining new mentors. Till this day I meet coaches and people who become my mentors and help me excel in other areas of life.

REMEMBER...

Failure is necessary for success.

THE NATURAL OLYMPIA
REAPING THE REWARDS OF HARD WORK AND VISION

The Natural Olympia is the most prestigious international natural bodybuilding competition in the world. Teams from all over the globe bring their best athletes and fly thousands of miles to compete in it. In 2016, the championship was held in Las Vegas in the big Rio Hotel arena. Teams from 60 countries were present.

Team USA Athletes

I was flying out to Vegas on Thursday morning. I woke up on Wednesday feeling kind of sick. I figured I was just sore and tired from all the training. But I continued to feel worse as the day went on. By the afternoon, I was running a fever, and the realization hit me that I had the flu! It hit me hard! I was very frustrated, because this was just two days before competition day!

The flu added another element of stress. Now, not only was I dealing with dehydration, fatigue, and competition stress, but also the flu. My body was going through hell, but my mindset and psychology were very strong. I kept visualizing myself standing on stage and winning the gold medal. I played motivational audios on a loop in order to keep my mental state elevated. I tried everything I could to stay strong.

A few days earlier, I had been in contact with the Jordanian Embassy in Washington DC. I told them that I was competing and they sent me a huge Jordanian flag for me to hold on the first-place podium. The flag arrived the day I flew out to Vegas, and that gave me a boost. I was excited that my country was also supporting me on this journey.

I'm always proud of Jordan and want to make my people proud—both my friends and family who were rooting for me to win, as well as all the immigrants who come to the United States with big dreams. I want to show them that with hard work, dedication, and immense passion, they can make it and achieve their dreams too.

The Jordanian flag was posted on the banner which had the flags of the countries that had contestants. I was the only Jordanian athlete competing with Team USA. There were around 70 athletes from the US alone.

It's showtime! This was the pinnacle of all my insane hard work and dedication. Now I had to go out and show the world what a Jordanian guy could accomplish in America!

Jordanian flag   I dialed down to 4% body fat

The pump-up began. There were hundreds of athletes back-stage. Among them was a friend of mine, Charles. Charles competed in the physically challenged category because of a genetic lung condition.

Charles

I'd met Charles for the first time some months earlier. I saw him working out with his oxygen tank. He would do sets, then take a breath from the tank, and then continue to work out like it was nothing. I was amazed that despite shortness of breath he came to compete and was in phenomenal shape. I was really inspired by him.

Charles is the perfect example of how powerful the human spirit is. With all the challenges he faces, he never complains, continues to train, and competes every year.

Even though my fever was worsening and my head was pounding, seeing Charles inspired me to get on stage and give it my all.

My closest competition was a Korean athlete, Kim. His physique was very close to mine. The difference would be down to maybe 0.1% body fat.

I had seen Tony Robbins do jumps to pump himself up just before he went on stage. So, minutes before we were called to go on stage I started jumping like crazy. They called our names to line up, and I walked on stage with complete confidence, like a lion walking toward an injured gazelle.

As I began my posing routine, the fever caused my body to shake, but I held myself with every ounce of energy left in me. At this point my heart and will took over.

The pose-down began!

In the 1970s Arnold's main competitor was a fellow named Sergio Oliva. They always battled for first place. As soon as Sergio did one pose, Arnold would do two and hype up the crowd. So I did the same.

Every time Kim hit a pose, I hit another, and the crowd would go wild.

It was a tough battle, but I left the auditorium thinking of nothing other than winning. I talked to my friends as if I'd already won. Self-doubt and negative talk still hit me, but I ignored all that. I kept visualizing myself on the podium receiving the gold medal. That was my only focus.

The waiting game to be crowned the Natural Olympia world champion was a big deal. Minutes felt like hours and the hours felt like days.

Finally, the judges were ready to announce the winners. They started calling out names.

"Third place, bronze medal, goes to Tom Keyburn!"

"The second place, silver medal, goes to . . . Kim Seungjoo."

"And the gold medal goes to WASIM HAJJIRI!!!"

Oh my God! I felt like . . . I don't even know how to explain how I felt. It was amazing, spectacular, like a dream. I was flying, soaring high in the sky! This was one of the best and happiest moments in my life. All the insane hard work that I put into this had paid off.

I had won the Olympia! The Olympics of natural body-building and fitness! Plus, the gold medal qualified me as a professional athlete—something I'd dreamed of since I was a kid!

Standing at the first-place podium with my mother
next to me and the Jordanian flag

The first thing I do is look for my mother. She's sitting in the front row, smiling, laughing, and cheering from her heart. We share a look that is worth every moment of the ten years that I committed to this sport. She comes toward the stage to hug me. She passes me the Jordanian flag so I can hold it high on the first-place podium. She has knee problems and needs help to get onto the stage. The judges kindly assist her. The first thing she does is hug the second- and third-place winners and congratulate them. I feel so proud in this moment to be my mother's son and share the great values she has.

My mother and me, after winning the gold medals

I can't help but wish that my father was with us. But I know he is in heaven looking down at me, smiling and cheering.

I'm so grateful that I had the chance to compete. It has been a long, tough journey. "Wasim worked really hard to win this," the judge announced after I received the gold medal, as they knew I had competed many times before coming here.

Everyone was congratulating me and giving me hugs. I genuinely felt all the love and respect in the INBA community. Even Kim and his Korean team came and congratulated my mother and me.

What I visualized in my head for over a year had come true. Even though I lost many times in the process of getting here, I always focused on winning, until it became my reality.

Gold medals 1   Gold medals 2

Olympia definition

KEY TAKEAWAY

The flu added an extra element of challenge and stress to the competition. When I was on that stage, I was drained physically and felt like dying, but mentally I was very strong. The aspects that helped me were my belief in winning, visualization of success, affirmations ("I will win no matter what!"), motivational audios, and physical movement (jumping elevates the mental state). My friends, family, and country were counting on me as well!

I wanted to win this from the bottom of my heart and soul. The purpose of winning was really deep for me; it wasn't about being under the spotlight, fame, money, or any of that. It was about making my father proud up there in heaven, making my mother proud. I wanted to make my country and people proud. I wanted to inspire people all over the world and show them that anyone can come to the US, start from scratch, and accomplish big things.

What I learned from Charles is that I should not complain about anything, appreciate what I have, and really go after what I want with absolutely no excuses! He had every reason to make excuses, but he didn't. He trained with his heart and soul, which is the true definition of a champion!

REMEMBER...

The purpose of winning was really deep for me
and that lit a fire in me that allowed me
to push through the tough times.

FIRST TIME ON TV
USING FAME TO INSPIRE OTHERS

Another dream that I had was to appear on live television. After winning three gold medals, I believed I had a strong story to share with the world, telling them about my journey from Jordan to the United States, starting a new life, and what it took to accomplish my dreams. I wanted to inspire people all over the world to take massive action toward their own dreams and believe that absolutely anything can be accomplished through hard work and dedication. This book formed from this powerful purpose.

I contacted every single news and radio station in San Diego. I sent hundreds of emails and made hundreds of cold calls. I wrote many different proposals and kept trying and adjusting. I was rejected or ignored over a hundred times.

My strategy was to never stop until I heard, "Yes, we will cover your story."

Slowly but surely, I got my first interview, and it was with FOX5 News.

They filmed the interview at my house. They took many pictures and videos of me training, and I told them my whole story. They aired the segment a week later, during prime viewing time. I was excited because Fox has a lot of viewers, and my interview aired during the presidential election campaign, so there were many people watching.

When the time came, my mother and I had our phone cameras at the ready as we anxiously waited for a whole hour before the show started.

Boom! There it was! I was looking at myself on TV.

After the segment was posted online, I got thousands more additional views.

FOX5

When it was over, I got random calls from people I hadn't seen in years congratulating me and telling me, "Oh man, we saw you on Fox News! What's going on?!" It was a dream come true!

After Fox, I went on a spree contacting other stations, and it worked! I appeared on CBS8 News, ABC10 News, Channel 10 News, and iHeartRadio. The Rady School of Management featured my story on their website. I worked hard to get my story out to these stations, and I faced rejection many times. But I never stopped believing that it would happen, and it eventually did.

ABC10

CBS8

When I visited Jordan, my family and friends threw a big celebration for me; it felt just like a parade. I then contacted the news stations there and appeared on Roya TV, which is the top station, and more than thirty magazines published my story.

Many people talked to me after these experiences and told me how sharing my story inspired them to act and believe that they are going to succeed. I believe that my life purpose is to help and inspire others around me. It is truly something that I enjoy and love.

You can watch the media clips on YouTube if you go to my channel: https://www.youtube.com/channel/UC8xtNgJJBxkNUXD7ngooUwA/videos

KEY TAKEAWAY

I believe that everyone and everything has a purpose. It took me some time before I realized that having an impact on others was my own life purpose.

Everyone has a purpose. Mine is to have an impact and inspire others.

19

WALKING ON FIRE
THE POWER OF MIND OVER BODY

March 23, 2017, was a day that changed my life. I attended the famous "Unleash the Power Within" seminar held by Tony Robbins. I'd been listening to Tony's audios daily for years and had read many of his books. He's had a huge positive impact on my life.

I walked into a huge auditorium packed with 9,000 people. It looked like I was attending a rock concert.

Attending "Unleash the Power Within" seminar

Music and lights were everywhere. The cheers, claps, and shouts filled the auditorium with crazy energy. It was an ecstatic and amazing feeling.

Finally, a tall, 6'7" man walks onstage, and the crowd goes insane. People start jumping and screaming as if he were a rock star! I can't even describe my feelings at this point, as I was immersed in the moment and enjoying every second of it. It was like a dream come true.

Every twenty minutes or so he would have us stand up, dance, jump, and clap, and he would blast some high-energy music. He taught us some breath exercises as well, and showed us how posture can affect our state.

He used drum sticks and slammed them together to pump up the crowd. He did this to keep everyone's physical and mental state at a great level. Even though I'd had only two hours of sleep the night before, all the movement and surrounding high energy kept me wide awake.

The main purpose of all the movement was to teach us how powerful our physiology is and how it affects the mind, including our emotions, energy, confidence, and overall performance. When we were in a peak state and he asked us questions, we answered much differently than we would have answered in a normal average state. Besides dancing, he led us all to interact with the people around us, hugging, giving high fives, and partnering in groups to do exercises. This created so much love and warmth in the atmosphere.

The high energy, positivity, and love everywhere was so strong that I felt it deep down in my heart. I had never experienced these feelings so intensely before, and it felt like sheer ecstasy.

The best part of the event for me was the fire walk. Before the event I saw videos where people were talking about their fire-walking experience. It looked completely insane, but I really wanted to do it and live the experience.

The purpose of the fire walk is to break you out of thinking or believing that something is impossible. Walking on fire was something I never thought I could do. I mean, come . . . on. It's fire! Coals of 2000-plus degrees. I was honestly scared out of my mind just thinking about it.

At around 11 p.m., Tony had been on stage for about twelve hours straight. I was wondering how he did it with no breaks. I never even saw him leave to go to the bathroom. He was speaking with all his heart and soul and still had so much energy. At 57, that is pretty impressive. He started preparing us for the fire walk. The first part of the prep was the pump-up.

He blasted high-energy music and everyone started jumping and dancing, while chanting "Yes, yes, yes" many times, which was a positive incantation used to lift up our spirits. Tony explained that the human brain can't distinguish between fantasy and reality, so when you visualize anything, the brain believes it and starts moving toward it. So he had us visualize the whole fire-walk process many times. To keep the brain away from the thought of falling or burning yourself, he taught us to repeat the phrase "cool moss," and instructed us to keep saying it while walking on the fire.

After an hour, we were pumped up and ready to do this. The auditorium emptied out, heading toward a nearby park where the fire lanes were set up. With 9,000 people moving from one location to another, the streets were closed, with police everywhere for protection. I thought, *Wow, downtown LA would only shut down its streets for a big shot like Tony.*

Fire walk

Everyone was chanting "Yes!" to keep the energy high and for group support. I was walking with some new friends I'd made, and we never stopped saying "Yes!" Bianca was my pump-up buddy. She had done the fire walk before and knew the experience, so she helped a lot. I was scared out of my mind, and my heart was pumping 100 times a minute.

As we got closer to the park, I started to freak out more and more in my head.

I'm going to fall and burn in front of all these people, I thought to myself. To remove that, I kept chanting "yes, yes, yes," and turned to talk to people around me and gave them high fives to pump them up.

No phones are allowed, because the flash could break people's focus while walking. I put my phone away and stood in the line. You would step onto a patch of wet grass while a coach pumped you up and made sure you were 100% ready to go before sending you across the burning coals.

This was right before we got in line for the fire walk

My heart was pounding faster. I was still chanting "Yes," but my mind was chanting "Oh no, you are going to burn." It was intense.

I watched the person in front of me walk across the fire. Seeing him do it made me feel a little better.

Now it was my turn . . .

I jumped on the grass, and instead of chanting, I started screaming like crazy, "Yes! Cool moss! Cool moss!" Then I thought, *Ahh ahh noo, ahh noo, I'm going to die!* The coach pumped me up even more. "One . . . two . . . three, GO!" she said. I didn't look down and started walking across the coals while imagining I was Superman. My adrenaline levels were sky high and I did not feel a thing.

It took about eight steps on the burning hot fire to reach the finish line. I did it! I saw Bianca and my other friends, and we hugged and celebrated like crazy. I was still shaking from the excitement. I have never done anything this crazy before. I felt like I was reborn.

Thinking about it later, I realized I had made the fire walk so big in my head and freaked out about burning myself, but it went by just fine and the final results were amazing. I noticed how I sometimes tend to make things so big in my head that it keeps me from acting or moving forward. It all ties back to some kind of fear.

My fire-walk experience shifted my mindset on taking action on anything in life. I decided to dump all the stories I create in my mind, the excuses, and just take massive action and walk on fire! I linked this experience to a new belief that I will live by every day: "The road to the goal might be 2000-degree burning hot coals (very difficult and filled with challenges), but in the end I will walk across this burning fire and succeed."

KEY TAKEAWAY

Tony really stresses controlling your physical and mental state and keeping yourself in peak form. I started to apply this to my normal everyday life. When I'm studying or working and sitting at my desk, I started taking a break every hour. I would stand up and do some jumps and a breath exercise that he taught. It would pump me up and help me focus better.

As I'm going through my day and I get angry, frustrated, or negative, I shift my physiology by doing a breath exercise. It gets me back to a better state. I noticed how powerful this is and made it a daily habit. This made me much more productive.

The fire walk taught me that I could take action despite being afraid. Fear tends to creep in from time to time, especially when I'm doing something big. A famous quote comes to mind: "Whatever we fear the most is what we really want to do." So many of us let our fear stop us. But courage is feeling the fear and taking action anyway.

REMEMBER...

Courage is feeling the fear
and taking action anyway.

FOR MORE INFORMATION/ RESOURCES

You can follow me on social media:

LinkedIn:
https://www.linkedin.com/in/wasim-hajjiri-mba-eng-2194b994/

YouTube:
https://m.youtube.com/channel/ UC8xtNgJJBxkNUXD7ngooUwA

Instagram:
https://www.instagram.com/wasimthedreamm/

Facebook:
Wasim Hajjiri

Twitter:
https://twitter.com/WasimTheDreamm

You can find all my products and services on my website: www.wasimthedream.com

Click on the link above to subscribe to my newsletter and get some freebies!

ACKNOWLEDGMENTS

I want to thank my amazing mother, who has been my number-one fan since I was young. She stood by my side through all the ups and downs in life and always encouraged me to be my best and succeed. Without her, none of my dreams, including this book, would have come to reality.

I want to thank my father, God bless his soul. He has always been my idol and a main source of inspiration. He taught me everything that I know about life and instilled in me the amazing values that he had that allowed me to become the person I am today.

I want to thank my best friends Mohammed Assaf and Suhail Romanos. We have been friends for more than ten years, and they have stuck by my side through all the ups and downs that I have been through in my journey toward my dreams.

I want to thank Bethany Kelly for being my publishing coach and mentoring me through this amazing journey of writing this book. I've been through many challenges along the way, and she kept me inspired and pushed me to write even when I didn't feel like it or got stuck. She truly made this dream become a reality.

I want to thank Liz Goodgold, who is my speaking and business coach. She helped me develop my speaking abilities and build my speaking business.

I want to thank dean Robert Sullivan. He is one of the most humble and passionate people that I have met. When I told him about my business idea and this book, he gave me a huge push to keep moving forward and think on a massive scale of how to positively impact and change the world. I hold his words dear to my heart.

I want to thank Herb Meistrich for being a phenomenal mentor. His incredible experience and genuine kindness allowed me to grow not just in business but in other areas of life.

149

I want to thank my coach and mentor Adnan Al Abbadi, who trained me for four years in Jordan before I moved to the US. He made me a better person and athlete.

I want to thank my coach Jeff Kotterman, who stuck by my side and helped me succeed in my competitive career in fitness.

I want to thank the Rady School of Management, including the administration staff, students, and professors for positively impacting my life. I think of them as my family. Rady helped me pursue my business ventures and turn many of my dreams into reality.

I want to thank my high school teacher Nabil Al Far, who became my first mentor. He changed my whole attitude about school and made me work hard, graduate, and get accepted into the engineering program.

I want to thank Eric the Trainer, who introduced me to my idols and people I'd watched on TV who I never thought I could see in real life. Thank you for inviting me to your gym and including me in your community.

I also want to thank all of my fellow Jordanians for supporting me throughout my journey.

ABOUT THE AUTHOR

Wasim Hajjiri is an electrical engineer with an MBA degree from the prestigious UCSD, Rady School of Management. He worked for two of the top tech companies globally, Qualcomm and Orange Telecommunications. He is a three-time gold medalist and top-five world class fitness athlete in the INBA (International Natural Bodybuilding Association) with ten years of weight-lifting experience. Wasim has six national and international TV appearances, including CBS8 News, FOX5 News, ABC10 News, Channel 10 News, iHeartRadio, Roya TV, INBA, TriSystem, and Go Natural Athlete. His story has been featured by UCSD, the Rady School of Management, and by more than 30 magazines in Jordan.